Hearts &Minds

A PUBLIC SCHOOL MIRACLE

Sandra Dean

VIKING

VIKING

Published by the Penguin Group

Penguin Books Canada Ltd, 10 Alcorn Avenue, Toronto, Ontario, Canada
M4V 3B2

Penguin Books Ltd, 27 Wrights Lane, London w8 5TZ, England

Penguin Putnam Inc., 375 Hudson Street, New York, New York 10014, U.S.A.

Penguin Books Australia Ltd, Ringwood, Victoria, Australia

Penguin Books (NZ) Ltd, cnr Rosedale and Airborne Roads, Albany, Auckland 1310,
New Zealand

Penguin Books Ltd, Registered Offices: Harmondsworth, Middlesex, England

First published 2000

10   9   8   7   6   5   4   3   2   1

Printed and bound in Canada on acid free paper   ∞

CANADIAN CATALOGUING IN PUBLICATION DATA

Dean, Sandra
    Hearts and minds: a public school miracle

ISBN 0-670-88982-2

1. South Simcoe Elementary School (Oshawa, Ont.). 2. Dean, Sandra. 3. Educational
change—Ontario—Oshawa. 4. Community and school—Ontario—Oshawa. 5. Education, Urban—Ontario—Oshawa. 6. Educational innovations—Ontario—Oshawa.
I. Reynolds, John Lawrence. II. Title.

LE5.O83D42 2000   372.9713'56   C00-931196-3

Visit Penguin Canada's web site at **www.penguin.ca**

To my husband, Ishwar,
for your love, belief, wisdom
and spiritual guidance

Contents

Introduction: A Message to the Reader

The children you will read about in this book are unique, as are all children; their experiences and achievements are theirs alone. But they have something in common with your own children, your neighbour's children and children living elsewhere in your community—this is vital to your understanding and appreciation of the story about to unfold on the following pages.

The children in your family and your neighbourhood may not endure the trials faced by many of the boys and girls whose stories you are about to encounter. Those to whom you are closest may be—and I pray they are—free from physical and emotional abuse, confident in the love and support of their families and enjoying a life of comfort and good health. Yet they, just like the kids from South Simcoe, are vulnerable, impressionable and struggling to understand and assume their role in the community.

Both these children and those in your own neighbourhood will eventually assume responsibility as adults. That is their common destiny. They will be your physician, your visiting homemaker, your care-giver and protector, your hope and trust for the future. In other words, their eventual role is to help you, and your current role is to assist them in meeting the challenges of being a child.

During the years I served as principal of South Simcoe Public School, I was privileged to spend time at what I do best and love most: teaching and working with children. I was also fortunate to do so with a dedicated team who shared my concern and commitment, and with community partners who gave generously of their time and their love. Together, our efforts helped the children of South Simcoe Public School to become more resilient.

The children of South Simcoe are not the only ones who needed this encouragement to earn a voice in their own society. The need exists among all children everywhere. It is a need that all of us should be prepared to fulfill with enthusiasm, with dedication and with love.

That is the message of South Simcoe Public School.

Chapter 1

A Dream Fulfilled

The thing I remember most clearly is the strange instant of silence just before my heart leaped at the news.

In that fraction of time, everything crystallized for me: the hopes, the frustrations, and the memories of so many tears and, yes, so much laughter too. During that brief moment they all became real again, and the crises and tragedies that often accompanied them were nowhere in sight.

Then the screaming and the shouting started—nineteen educators, two police officers and one director of education, all of us a thousand miles from home, leaping on the spot, holding hands, hugging and laughing, while others in the hall smiled with pleasure at our unbridled joy.

It was April 1995, and South Simcoe Public School, which three years earlier had suffered the humiliation of posting the worst student marks of all the schools in its region, had just won a national award for Excellence in Business and Education Partnerships from the Conference Board of Canada. What's more, the travel expenses for the staff members who accompanied us to the ceremony in Saint John, New Brunswick, had been paid by donations from local residents and business people who believed in us and all we had set out to do for the students of South Simcoe Public School.

But I wasn't thinking of that as we all crowded onto the platform to accept the prize and acknowledge the standing ovation from the audience. No Academy Award–winning celebrities ever felt greater pride and excitement than we did at that moment. We had managed to prove something vital about education, first to our students, then to their parents and community, and now to the entire country and beyond.

How far we have come, I thought, watching the staff celebrate that evening in Saint John. Of course, we had had so far to travel from that first day. But only when the journey is so great can the progress be measured with such giant steps.

Becoming principal of my own school had been a dream of mine almost from the first day I chose teaching as a career. It's not an unusual ambition, I suspect. Every teacher dedicated to making a positive impact on students, and prepared to challenge the usual way of doing things, thinks from time to time about being appointed principal. In early 1991 the position was offered to me. However, when I discovered that my school would not be a neat and tidy suburban one, furnished with shining facilities and peopled by solidly middle-class students, but a tired, seventy-five-year-old inner-city school that probably faced closure, I admit my heart sank a little.

Built when schools were considered part monument and part institution, the structure was small and dark, its brown brick walls crowned with stone and concrete in a style that reminded me of pictures of Queen Victoria glaring at the camera, stern and forebidding. Its location, directly across the street from a strip mall, was a principal's nightmare. The teachers at South Simcoe faced enormous difficulties as a result of these and other factors. The proof was evident: of all eighty-nine schools within the Durham District School Board, South Simcoe Public School was poorest when it came to measuring student performance levels in reading, writing and mathematics.

Yet, within a short number of years, South Simcoe Public School would rise to the top of all schools in its district. Not just higher, or among the best of its group, or even among the top ten—it would sit at the very summit, *with 100 percent of its students performing at the highest levels in the same subjects in which it had fared poorest.*

This is the story of its journey from Worst to First. It was not always smooth or swift, and from time to time we encountered a pothole or two along the way. But, oh, how rewarding the trip was for everyone... especially the children!

When I first learned that I would be stepping up to the role of principal at a school within my district, I was naturally pleased and excited. Promotion to a principal's position is more than recognition of your abilities and experience; it represents an opportunity to shape a school by touching the hearts and minds of children, in a manner no other profession can offer. As a parent, you can influence your own children. As a teacher, you affect the lives of perhaps twenty-five or thirty children in your care each day. But as a principal, you have the opportunity to make a positive impact on literally hundreds of children and improve their lives in at least some small way. Me, a principal? I could hardly wait to get started. Just tell me where!

To say that I had mixed emotions when the answer came back "South Simcoe Public School" is something of an understatement. In fact my first reaction was immediately negative. "I don't want to go there," I said to my superintendent, Carol, when she called me at home with the news. For as long as anyone could remember, South Simcoe was located on "the wrong side of the tracks." This is more than a cliché in industrial Oshawa, where economic and social conditions are clearly stratified. "It's an old school, they're going to close it soon, and it's not my kind of place." Those were three pretty good reasons to send somebody else, I believed.

"Sandra, South Simcoe *is* your kind of place," my superintendent replied. "The children need someone like you. You can make a difference there. Look, I promise if you go there you'll shine." She must have sensed that I remained unconvinced, because she added, "If, in a few months, you still feel you would rather go somewhere else, we'll talk about it."

Naturally, I agreed. I really wanted to be a principal, after all.

One of the things all educators discover is that you never stop learning. There are lessons to be gained from virtually everything you experience as a teacher. Certainly, over my seven and a half years as principal at South Simcoe Public School, I absorbed many lessons, and the first came from my own family on the very day I was told of my appointment.

"We're so proud of you," my husband, Ishwar, said. My sons, Shiva and Rishi, along with other family members, added their congratulations. But the expression on my face, and my own self-doubts, became immediately apparent.

"I'm not sure I can handle it," was my reply. The truth was, I felt more than doubt; I felt disappointment as well. Like every profession, teaching has its share of prestigious positions, and being principal of a school like South Simcoe was not one of them.

"Of course you can," Ishwar said. "You'll make a great principal. You have the training, the experience, and most of all the attitude to deal with kids who need care and attention. It's the best place for you."

"It's kind of dreary," I said. "You know how those older school buildings are. Not much light, dull colours, huge hallways, and—"

"Then we'll help you fix things up," Ishwar said. "The boys and I will pitch in before the school year starts. A little paint and some wallpaper can make a big difference, you know that. Besides," he added in a more serious tone, "it's not the building that needs your talents, it's the children."

This initial lesson, of course, taught me that I wasn't alone. I enjoyed the total support of my family, and the support base grew to encompass first the teaching staff and school custodian, then the parents, local merchants, service clubs, the police department and finally the entire community. Ishwar was absolutely correct. I was not alone, and in no way could I have accomplished as much as I did without the support of this ever-widening circle of people who worked with me to make a difference.

Many of my beliefs about raising and educating children are hardly new, such as the idea that children are to be valued and nurtured in order to bring out the best in them. Their precious spirit stems, in my opinion, from their innocence and vulnerability. We all know that these two qualities dissipate with the passage of time and the experience of living; that's part of the process of maturing into an adult. But too many children lose them too early and in the wrong way, through abuse, neglect and the oppression of social conditions.

I have yet to encounter a troubled child who could not

benefit from healthy doses of love and care. For some reason a few members of our society believe that individuals in the two extremes of life, childhood and old age, either don't require or don't deserve our full attention. How can this be? Why can't children enjoy the same degree of dignity and respect that we demand for ourselves? Imagine for a moment that you are no longer as independent as you are today. You can be either a child or an elderly invalid—it works either way—and you are under the control of someone stronger than yourself, someone who seeks to dominate you with threats and punishment. How would you feel?

Control and manipulation of children are ultimately doomed to failure. I saw proof of this during my years of teaching, in my position as vice-principal and, of course, in my experience as a parent. I sincerely believe that the best method of educating children is, first, to love and care for them and, above all, to believe in them; and second, to provide them with ways of increasing their own sense of self-worth, enabling them to experience the joy and satisfaction that comes from accomplishing something and doing it well. You don't teach a child to ice-skate, for example, by threatening punishment if she doesn't learn how to keep her ankles stiff. You demonstrate and encourage. You praise and support. You do not threaten. And when you experience the delight on a child's face as she finally masters such a skill, you share in her pleasure and pride.

Does this mean that *any* behaviour is acceptable in children? Of course not. As adults we recognize the sense of responsibility expected from us as members of society. Physical assaults, theft, disturbances and similar behaviours are simply not acceptable. But neither, I believe, should they be dealt with simply by punishment. It is not that easy. It is *never* that easy, as almost anyone in our justice system will agree.

These ideas represented the core of my beliefs while I prepared myself to assume the role of principal at South Simcoe Public School, the first step in a journey that led to all the whooping and excitement in New Brunswick, and beyond.

Looking back on it, I realize that my career could have taken one of two very different routes. The one that I originally longed to travel would have been smooth and paved, across generally flat terrain. I would have followed this route as principal of a bright and shiny school in a wealthy suburb, a school populated by students whose minds were filled as much (or, let's face it, more!) with visions of new fashions and the sounds of new music as with the lessons at hand. Such a journey would require little passion and energy from me.

The other route was uncertain and rocky, traversing new territory and climbing from a deep valley up steep canyon walls, ever upwards, stumbling from time to time, with the ever-present risk of falling to disaster. Finishing the trek would test my abilities as an educator and strengths as a person, and require large reserves of nerve, energy and belief in myself and an entire team. But at the end, if we succeeded, we would all stand higher and prouder than we began.

That's the route I took when I agreed to become principal of South Simcoe Public School. I did it because I knew I had the support of my family, my friends, my colleagues and my school board.

"Did I do something wrong?" I asked Ruth Lafarga the day after I learned I had been assigned to South Simcoe. Ruth chaired the school board and was the trustee of the area that included the school. As much as anyone, she knew the challenges facing South Simcoe . . . and me.

"No, of course not," she said, laughing. "I *want* someone like you there."

That was my second lesson. I wasn't being sent to South Simcoe merely out of convenience. I was being challenged to put all my values and beliefs into action, where they would do the most good for the most people.

Well, I thought, hanging up the telephone, we might as well get started.

Chapter 2

The Task I Was Meant to Do

*W*hen I am asked about the source of the ideas and concepts we used at South Simcoe Public School, I realize that many of them have their roots in my experiences growing up in Trinidad, and most were part of me by the time I was ten years old.

Trinidad is a country similar to Canada in some ways, yet very different in others. The climate and geography of the two countries could not be more different, and the total area of Trinidad and Tobago is much less than that of Prince Edward Island, Canada's smallest province. Perhaps as a result of the population density, people in Trinidad and other Caribbean islands find it natural to extend their hand to others without being asked. I loved living in this environment as a child, and when I became an educator I wanted to recreate the village environment and the extended-family concept in my teaching role.

My clearest childhood memories in Trinidad are of my father, who actively sought out those who were in need and found a way to provide assistance. Instead of waiting to be asked for help, he would travel to villages far beyond our own city, looking for ways he could make people's lives easier. As a young child I often accompanied my father on these journeys, and I was constantly struck by the difference between the lives of those he encountered and my own. Our family was solidly upper middle class. We enjoyed luxuries and never wanted for food, shelter or security. Meeting people who were desperately in need of support, and watching my father find ways to help solve their problems, made him something of a miracle worker in my eyes.

When I asked my father why some of these people did not have enough to eat or a comfortable place to live, as we did, he explained that they had no money to purchase those things.

"Why don't they just go out and make the money they need?" I asked.

"That is why I try to help them," my father replied. "So that they can find ways of improving their existence."

It was a simple and honest response, but an important one to me. My father did not believe in simple handouts of food and other items from those, such as our own family, who had resources to share. He wanted people to help themselves, I believe, because along with the material benefits they would also experience pride in their achievement. I have never met anyone who takes pride in being handed food, money or clothing and told, in effect, to go away. And I have never failed to notice the pleasure felt by people, especially children, when they achieve something that they and others once believed was beyond their reach. That kind of pride can literally change people forever, and it lasts longer than any free meal or a hand-me-down garment.

I suppose I was especially impressed by my father's

concern for others because it made me realize how privileged our family was in many ways. As the eldest child in our family, I may have been the most privileged of all.

The significance of family ties and the importance of education reigned supreme in our home. Our ancestors had emigrated to Trinidad from India, where wisdom and knowledge were considered among the greatest treasures anyone could acquire. They arrived in the mid-nineteenth century after slavery had been abolished on the island and cheap labour was needed to harvest the sugar crops. Even as fieldworkers they retained an appreciation for the value of education and a respect for the wisdom gained over a lifetime.

I was continually reminded of the importance of education by my grandmother, who, ironically, never attended school (which I realize now was a lesson in itself). During her childhood years education for girls had been considered a waste. Beyond knowing how to sew, cook, clean house and deliver babies, what other skills did a woman need? That was how people thought in the early twentieth century. In quiet rebellion, my grandmother taught herself to count, a skill she used when selling vegetables from the small garden she planted and tended, and she expected all her grandchildren, boys and girls alike, to obtain all the education they could absorb.

In my grandmother's view, happiness and education were permanently entwined. "You've got to find out why you were placed on this earth," she would tell us. "You've got to find the task you were meant to do and choose a path to take. Then you'll find true happiness and peace. We are all here to do something special. It is up to you to discover what it is."

I spent my early school days in a private convent school, where the teaching nuns were kind and caring, creating a sense of family among us. The sisters had high expectations for their students, and firmly instilled a strong sense of self-discipline in us. If something needed to be done by a certain time, at a certain level of skill, we were expected to achieve it. If we did not, we were encouraged to keep trying and not simply give up.

There were times when I and other students at the convent school doubted our ability to do something, whether mastering a new algebra method or completing a reading assignment. But the sisters were always convinced that we could do it, and they managed to pass this belief on to us. I cannot overemphasize the value of this lesson to a child, even a child such as myself who was constantly being told by her parents that I could achieve anything I wanted to if I wanted it badly enough. It is important for everyone—parents, teachers and the entire community—to believe in the potential of children.

For our twenty-fifth wedding anniversary, Ishwar and I travelled to France. There I met my retired school principal, Sister Marie Joseph, who had taken a special interest in me back at that convent school in Trinidad. I wanted to let her know how much she had influenced me, and how many of my successes owed their beginnings to her interest in me. She had encouraged me to read books, not just for knowledge but for the sheer joy of reading (she actually introduced me to Nancy Drew!). She had made me feel good about myself as a student and as an individual, and encouraged me to be courageous and take risks. She was kind and caring, and while I don't know if I meant any more to her than anyone else, *I felt that I did.* That was the key to all that I have carried with me from my school days. She made me feel valued, *and it made all the difference to me and who I have become.* That was why, so many years after I left the convent school, I wanted to meet that woman again. I wanted her to see that her trust and belief had not been misplaced in me. I went to France to do it. I would have travelled much farther if I had to.

We were told that you never lose what is placed in your head through education. Knowledge enables you to think for yourself and care for yourself. This idea of a treasure you carry in your own head is probably why a lot of families in Trinidad aspired to higher education—because it has a value of its own that can never fade.

At home, my parents never allowed anything to intrude seriously on our education. If we had a school test, or homework or an assignment to complete for the following day, our family would not plan a social event for that evening. School work came first, and that was that.

Family ties in Trinidad are extensive and powerful, and we saw our family members every weekend. Socializing is not something you do to pass the time or fulfill an obligation. It is as much a part of your life as the work you perform—perhaps more so.

Social obligations began with our immediate family. My mother insisted on all of us eating a good breakfast and enjoying healthy meals during the day. We were always expected to eat together, sharing stories of our day with each other across the dinner table. Naturally, holidays were celebrated with great joy and much tradition. On Christmas Day my father and his four brothers would visit their grandmother with their children, even great-great-grandchildren in later years. These were wonderful times. We shared news and gossip, each of us knowing that we enjoyed the support of one another in time of need.

And it wasn't a one-way street between the generations. My grandmother travelled regularly, spending a week with each of her children and grandchildren, ensuring everyone was all right. She even visited me in Canada when my son Rishi was born, spending a week with me and her newest grandchild as her way of helping me, and letting me know she loved and cared about me. It's the kind of thing mothers and grandmothers did in our family. Her journeys reflected the same kind of attitude my father displayed when he reached out to see who needed assistance in a far-off village. You didn't wait for someone to arrive on your doorstep pleading for help; you went looking for ways to provide it.

There were other lessons to be learned as well. I remember one year when, as a young girl, I discovered a special fascination for dolls. I wanted not just ordinary dolls but *special* dolls—large and lifelike, dressed in fancy clothing. One Christmas I received just such a doll from my parents, and I thought it was the most fabulous of its kind in all of Trinidad.

That same Christmas, a visitor to our home brought his brother along to meet us. Friends and family always made a point of visiting during the Christmas season, and tradition held that visitors were always welcome to bring friends or relatives with them to share the joy of the season. The brother was kind enough to bring a gift for me.

When I unwrapped the gift in front of the visitor, I discovered it was a doll. The doll was pleasant enough, but it couldn't compare with the large, elaborate doll my parents had given me. "Oh," I said, "another doll," and I set it aside.

My mother immediately suggested I come to the kitchen to assist her with the meal preparation. Of course she didn't need my help at all. I was the one in need—of a lesson.

"That young man took a lot of time and put a lot of care into choosing that doll just for you," she said, after setting me down in a chair. "He told me that he wanted you to have a special gift. You should accept it with the same amount of love and care he put into selecting it for you. So when you go back into the room, you need to pick up the doll, walk over to him, thank him for it and find something beautiful to say about it."

I think I may have pouted a little. "But it's not as nice as my other dolls," I said. "I don't like it."

"I know you can find something good to say about the doll," she told me. "Look carefully at it until you do. Then you go and thank him for it properly, and give him a hug to show you mean it."

As usual, my mother was pleasant but firm. So I returned to the living room and examined the doll more closely. The hair, I saw, was quite nicely done. So I carried it to the boy and said, "Thank you for my doll. I like her curly hair."

His reaction was immediate. His eyes lit up with joy and he reached out to hug me. "I'm glad you like it," he said. "I was so afraid that I might choose a gift for you that you didn't like."

I have never forgotten the feeling this gave me. Or the lessons it taught me. I learned that all gifts should be received with gratitude and love, and that we must avoid hurting the feelings of others. I also learned that, if you look hard enough, you will discover beauty or some special quality in much of life.

Childhood is filled with such lessons. I was fortunate

because virtually all of my lessons were positive ones, and I am often surprised at how many I have managed to apply in my life. They include:

- Help others give a gift of love each day; giving of yourself and your time brings happiness to others.
- Respect yourself; you are unique and special.
- Children are heavenly gifts. They are precious, and filled with love, joy and goodness. Nurture them, care about them and, above all, believe in them, and they will blossom and follow their own unique paths.
- Have the wisdom to value the gifts you carry within you.
- Everything you do—every small gesture, every act you perform—creates a ripple that affects someone else. So always act in a loving and respectful way.
- Family makes everyone stronger. Look after those who do not have their own family. This brings great joy and fulfilment.
- Everyone has value, worth and a role to play. The world is like a giant puzzle that needs all the pieces in order to be complete. One person is no more or no less important than another. Learn to share.

For most of my life I probably did not analyze these lessons in this manner; I simply applied them from instinct. But that's the point: they were so deeply rooted in me that I cannot be separated from these values any more than I can be separated from a part of my body, and this has helped me to help other parents and teachers understand the importance of these values.

These lessons would prove just as valid to the children

of South Simcoe Public School as they were to me. They represent the core of all that my staff and I, supported by an enlightened school board, created and applied to make such a remarkable difference to our students.

At age nineteen, my life changed in three significant ways: I graduated from the University of the West Indies with a degree in sociology and political science, Ishwar and I were married, and we emigrated to Canada—all within a few exciting months.

Ishwar was continuing his studies in electronic physics at the University of Western Ontario in London, Ontario. The special atmosphere of a university campus made our transition from Trinidadian to Canadian life a little easier, because so many people we encountered on the university campus were also from somewhere else. This did not make our first Christmas together much easier, however. We both missed our families very much, a feeling not even the beauty of the first heavy snowfall and the support of many new friends could alleviate.

The birth of our two sons quickly plunged me into all the activities of motherhood. Things changed, of course, often in ways I did not immediately recognize. Until then I had had little interest in furthering my education. But the sight of my children playing, sleeping, yearning to learn and reacting to life itself, sparked something in me. I realized I wanted to make a difference to kids in the same manner that many people had made a difference to me as a child.

I decided that teaching would offer the best opportunity. I was especially drawn to the idea of teaching young children who were hampered with difficulties of some kind. I knew that the biggest changes were often made during the earliest

years, and that children with learning disabilities needed special kinds of help.

Incidentally, becoming a teacher after earning a degree in
sociology and political science is not as much of a leap as
some people may think. My political studies had reaffirmed
my belief in democracy, and if you advocate that concept of
government, you must also assume that everyone has the
capacity to become whoever they choose to be. It also means
that you believe everyone has a role to play in the overall
scheme of things. These represent not only the essence of
democracy, in my opinion; they are also the basis of an effective approach to education.

So, with the enthusiastic support of my husband, I
obtained my teaching certificate and began my career by
working with children who suffered from mental handicaps.
From there I progressed through a series of public schools
until, by 1991, I had achieved vice-principal status at a school
in an affluent area of Whitby, Ontario, about thirty miles east
of Toronto. In 1991, I also began teaching the principal's
course at the University of Toronto's Ontario Institute for
Studies in Education (OISE), and later at York University.
These sessions, in evenings, on weekends and during the
summer months, helped me to retain a view of the wider
challenges of education, especially from the level of a
principal. I remained aware of much of the ongoing research
on the subject and naturally began considering the kinds of
programs I might initiate as a principal.

"You should be a principal," my husband would frequently suggest to me.

I would reply that I certainly hoped to be, someday. "Then
I'll be able to apply a lot of my own ideas," I would add.

Only when I discovered that my long-dreamed-of appointment was to be principal of South Simcoe Public School did my confidence waver. "Be careful about what you wish for," I recalled having read years earlier, "because it may come true."

Well, my wish had come true, in a sense. Now I had to prove I really wanted it—prove it to my family, my staff, the board officials who recommended me, and most of all, to myself.

Chapter 3
· · · · · ·

"Mother Bird"
Feathers Her Nest

As familiar as I was with South Simcoe Public School
and the challenges faced by its staff and students, I had never
set foot inside the building. When, among the many con-
gratulatory messages I received, one came from the woman
I was replacing as principal, I quickly accepted her invitation
to visit.

The steady roar of traffic, speeding west to Toronto
and east towards Montreal on nearby Highway 401, is a
constant reminder of the transient nature of the South
Simcoe neighbourhood. And it's not just the traffic that
is constantly in motion. About half of the families whose
children attended the school moved in or out of the area
each year, an astonishing rate of turnover. Whatever the reasons for this steady migration, and there were several, the
effect on young children of this repeated coming and going
of neighbours and friends was often devastating. Add the
familiar problems of other inner-city schools, such as family
disintegration, high unemployment, spousal abuse, drug and
alcohol abuse and more, and it's no surprise that the local

public school was often a maelstrom of rebellion, aggression, vandalism and failed dreams.

The building itself seemed to reflect the despair.

The square, brown-brick building squatted on a low, bare rise. I remember especially the barren ground and the peeling paint on the window frames. When built in 1916, South Simcoe Public School had sat amid the homes of proud factory workers, many of them recent immigrants employed at the giant General Motors automotive plant. Over the decades since, most of the more stable families abandoned the area in favour of middle-class suburban comfort. Property values nosedived and many homes in the area became stopovers for transient families.

The school became more than a casualty and a symptom of this decline. From the outside, South Simcoe Public School held little promise that anything positive could happen beneath its roof.

I left my car within sight of several bored teenagers who were smoking in the mall directly across the street.

Inside, the school maintained its rather sad appearance. Much of it was due, of course, to the old building's basic structure, dating back to a much earlier period of architectural design and educational environment. The school's library was minuscule, and as for the gymnasium—well, there *was* no gymnasium, and that was that. The staff gathered in a converted coal bunker in the cellar and, just to make things more annoying, the only staff washroom was up three steep flights of stairs.

My attention was quickly diverted from the building to the students. I had acquired a habit of always smiling at children in my roles as teacher and vice-principal. It put them at ease and helped dissolve the barriers created between students and staff. When I smiled at the children I passed on my way to the principal's office, the smiles I received back from them were more spontaneous and intense than I had become accustomed to at my suburban school. Their entire faces seemed to light up, as though they had been waiting for me to arrive and express pleasure at seeing them.

Naturally, I couldn't help commenting on it when the outgoing principal graciously welcomed me into the school and escorted me into her office. She wasn't surprised at my reaction.

"The kids here are truly wonderful," she told me. "They appreciate every bit of attention you give them, and that's what keeps me going some days."

Of all the discoveries I made that day, her comment about the need of these children for attention and support was the most encouraging. You can't, after all, blame a community for the troubles that occur in and around it. Nor can you blame a teaching staff faced with the challenge of teaching children whose minds may be diverted by empty stomachs, strife between their parents, neglect and abuse.

The fact is, I didn't believe in placing blame at all. Blame would not help me to provide the children with breakfast, resolve their insecurity and fear of failure, or comfort them when the world seemed hostile and unforgiving. It is an essentially useless exercise, a waste of energy and time. I hadn't been sent there to do that, I knew. I was there to do the best job I could for the children, and the brilliance of the smiles I received on my way to the principal's office made me more determined than ever to achieve my goal.

During the rest of the day I chatted one-on-one with the teachers at South Simcoe and discovered, to my surprise, that most of them enjoyed their time at the school. Sure, the old building was inefficient, even depressing sometimes. And creating a bond with parents was especially difficult because so many families moved in and out of the neighbourhood so often, and those who remained frequently did not feel confident enough in their own academic skills to help their children with homework and projects.

"Then what is it that gives you so much enjoyment here?" I kept asking, and over and over the answer came back: "The children."

I left South Simcoe convinced that I could make a difference. I had the support of my family and my school board behind me, plus my years of training and experience. Most of all, I would be helping children whose needs were so compelling that I felt I simply *must* apply my very best efforts to make a difference.

I was no longer dwelling on the question of whether my appointment to South Simcoe was a good thing or a bad thing. I was no longer hearing those voices. Instead, I was hearing my father's voice. "Don't wait for others to ask for help," I could hear him saying. "Reach out and help them."

And my grandmother's voice echoed as well. *You've got to find the task you were meant to do, and choose a path to take. Then you'll find happiness.*

I realized that all my training and good intentions would not be enough to change South Simcoe into the kind of school I envisioned. I spent a good deal of time researching reference material on inner-city schools, assisted by Professor Ken Leithwood, a friend and mentor from the Ontario Institute for Studies in Education at the University of Toronto. As we quickly discovered, the problems of inner-city schools in Canada and the impact of family trauma on children were well documented by statistics. We also uncovered much general information on education problems experienced by kids in these situations, and the impact of poverty and domestic conflict on society as a whole. But there was little on solutions, best practices and strategies for Canadian schools.

I moved from the general to the specific: what could I discover about South Simcoe from its records? The answer was devastating, and once again my roller-coaster ride of emotions took a nose-dive.

Poring over records provided by the previous principal, I discovered that the attendance rates for South Simcoe Public School were disappointing, as were the academic scores of its students—although on two occasions a child from South Simcoe had won Student of the Year recognition. Schoolyard fighting and bullying were a continual problem. Complaints of disrespect to school staff and local residents were ongoing, and the students were responsible for a high incidence of vandalism and shoplifting in the mall across the street.

But I kept remembering the words of the principal and teachers, and the sudden bright smiles on the faces of the boys and girls I encountered on my visit there. If there are problems, I thought, they certainly don't begin with the children.

When summer vacation arrived, I continued making major changes. I remembered how, as a child, I had looked forward to my hours at school. School was a bright, pleasant place to be, among adults who, despite whatever frustrations they may have experienced, really wanted to be there. That summer I recruited friends and family to add some finishing touches and turn the school into a bright, cheerful and welcoming setting for the children.

One of my friends, Wendy, volunteered to make curtains

for the windows. She needed accurate measurements but could only accompany me to the school during evening hours. The outgoing principal had warned me against visiting the school at night. Not only did we risk returning to our cars to discover the tires slashed or the paint scratched, but incidents of serious violence were not unknown. In fact someone was stabbed in the neighbouring strip mall the month I assumed my new position at the school.

So we were already a little nervous when we entered the darkened school late one evening. The custodial staff had left hours earlier and the old building was strangely quiet, with dark corners that threatened to conceal all sorts of perils and menace.

Wendy was standing on a chair holding a measuring tape to the window, and I was dutifully writing down the dimensions she called out to me, when I distinctly heard footsteps in the darkened hall beyond the room.

"Listen!" I hissed.

We stood frozen to the spot as the footsteps approached, heavy and threatening.

Had I locked the front door behind us? I wondered. I was sure I had.

The footsteps stopped, and we heard a door open and close down the hall. Wendy and I looked at each other, holding our breath and trembling a little. The traffic moving outside seemed so remote now. No one would hear us if we screamed.

"We have to see who it is," I whispered.

The footsteps resumed. They were definitely coming closer.

"I can't let you go alone," Wendy said. "I'll come with you." She had been using a hammer to place small nails in the window frame, and now she seized it like a weapon.

We both crossed the room and opened the door to the hall, Wendy with the hammer raised and me attempting to hide my fear, with little success.

Several feet away, a man confronted us.

"What are you doing here?" I said in my sternest principal voice.

"What am *I* doing here?" he said. "What are *you* doing here?"

I couldn't believe his arrogance. "I am here because I am the principal of this school and I am doing some work," I said in my most authoritative voice. "Now explain who you are."

"I'm the head of security," he said, "and you obviously didn't turn the alarm off when you came in."

All three of us laughed with relief before the man gave me a rather stern lecture on the importance of disarming the security system correctly when entering the building, especially late at night.

I sensed this would not be the last frightening incident I would encounter at South Simcoe. And, of course, it was not.

My appointment to South Simcoe coincided with the school's seventy-fifth anniversary, and some funds were made available to spruce up the old building in recognition of this milestone. The outgoing principal continued to be gracious and welcoming, and we spent a good deal of time talking to staff and visiting other area schools in search of decorating ideas.

Perhaps it's my Caribbean heritage, but I have always appreciated the ability of colour to set a mood. In Trinidad, colours are vibrant and exciting, and it's a joy to wear clothing in rich reds and bright yellows. I felt that the school needed an elegant backdrop for the children's artwork and other displays. Brilliant colours can always be applied here and there in the classroom; the feeling I wanted everyone to experience when first entering South Simcoe was one of welcome and warmth. We narrowed the colours down, then asked the staff to make a final choice. They selected an off-white finish for the walls with country-blue trim, and the result was perfect.

Among other changes I made was to relocate the principal's office, keeping it on the same floor as a Grade One classroom. This was, I must confess, a purely emotional decision on my part. I wanted to be near loving hugs and smiles provided by "my little darlings," as I called the youngest students, and I wanted to hear them singing together. There are few greater joys to a teacher than the voices of a Grade One class joined in song, lustily and joyfully. I expected to encounter frequent challenges to my normal optimistic state, days when I would feel weighted down with doubts and decisions. On those days I knew my spirits would be lifted by the sound of young voices singing in a room down the hall, and if I needed an emotional lift I could always drop in to read stories, or dispense and receive warm hugs.

In the remaining days and weeks before I welcomed the children on the first day of their school year at South Simcoe, I focused much of my attention on creating a special climate within the school, and the new paint and bright curtains were just the beginning. I wanted more than an environment for learning. I wanted an ambience that wrapped the staff and the children in positive feelings, as though the school represented the very best place they could be. I wanted the children to encounter reminders of their value and potential everywhere in the school, affirmations that they could make choices to change their lives in the direction they wished to travel. I wanted them to anticipate Monday mornings and rejoice in their return to the school. I wanted them to feel safe and secure within its walls, and know that they would look back on their years at South Simcoe and remember them as exciting, fulfilling and memorable.

All of this may make the school sound more like a loving home than a place for learning, but that is what I felt the children needed.

With the principal's office relocated, I moved the kindergarten to a larger room and found some money in the budget for new toys and furniture. We carpeted the floor, added plants and obtained rocking chairs for the teachers to sit in as they read books to the children gathered around to listen. Does a rocking chair help a teacher read better? Probably not. Does it add a sense of warmth and security for the children who are listening to the story? Somehow it does, and that's all that counted.

I didn't neglect the staff either, relocating their lounge out of the basement and onto the main floor. Instead of a dingy refuge, it became a place for sharing ideas, consultation, celebration and laughter, and it was also more accessible to parents.

Through the balance of the summer we transformed South Simcoe Public School into Cinderella prepared for the ball. Over the Labour Day weekend, just hours before the children were to begin their new school year, Ishwar, Shiva, Rishi and I were busy hanging wallpaper in the staff room and adding plants and attractive posters. It was important, I believed, for the renovation to be completed before the students arrived. Children arrive on the first day of school looking their best, and I wanted the school to reflect all the pride and optimism they were feeling.

The involvement of parents, I determined from a very early stage, would be absolutely critical. No matter how attractive the school became and how dedicated the staff were, none of the goals I envisioned could be reached without the support of parents. We needed total co-operation—not just periodic attendance at school events, but regular involvement in day-to-day activities, including decision-making and problem-solving. Did this mean parents could take an active role in the learning process? Well, why not?

I wanted to make parents and visitors feel welcome at South Simcoe, so I suggested during a staff meeting that we add a coffee machine in the staff room, and offer parents and visitors a cup of coffee. Someone asked who would pay for the coffee.

"I will," I replied.

Someone else noted that parents might come in just to enjoy a free cup of coffee.

I doubted this would always be the case, but if that's what it took to bring parents into the school, I had no problem with the idea. Eventually we installed not only a coffee machine but a large selection of teas and a cooler dispensing spring water.

We needed the students to recognize that the changes at South Simcoe were not limited to brighter colours and new decor. We wanted to show that changes had taken place beneath the surface as well, so I proposed a few critical ones at my first meeting with the teaching staff.

"We are role models in the way we dress and speak," I reminded them. The students, I added, needed to see us dressing, speaking and behaving according to the same standards we expected from them. This led to a series of agreements including one that jeans and track suits would not be worn by teachers and staff. (We did, however, implement "South Simcoe Days" on Fridays, when everyone on staff wore a South Simcoe Public School T-shirt or sweatshirt. What a sight it was to see everyone—teachers, principal and custodial staff—all decked out in the school colours!)

We also agreed that teachers would greet the children with a smile and a pleasant "Good morning!" or "Good afternoon!" as they arrived. Other staff members, including me, would be positioned on the stairs or landings so that, from the time the children walked through the school door and into their classroom, they would be greeted at least three times by a smiling adult and a friendly word. This reflected my personal heritage. In Trinidad, I remembered being expected to greet everyone with a smile and a friendly word, and this seemed like a worthwhile custom to introduce to South Simcoe.

Another agreement dealt with the manner in which we would address the children. Teaching is a very rewarding profession, but it can also become frustrating at times. If we were going to ask the children to respect us and each other, we needed to model this same behaviour when dealing with them. Thus, we agreed never to raise our voices in anger at the students.

We were, of course, restructuring the way we were dealing with behavioural problems, and it would not always be easy for teachers to retain their focus on this goal. If anger developed between a staff member and a student, the student could always cool down in my office. This approach was vital to achieving our goal of treating children with the dignity and respect they needed if they were to be respectful themselves. It also provided the children with a sense of safety and security, and an awareness that they were loved and cared for. All of this creates an environment for learning; teaching is always more successful when children feel safe and are undistracted by emotional concerns.

As educators, we couldn't change the home conditions or the state of the community around the school any more than we could change the underlying causes of many of these problems. Neither, of course, could the children. But we could provide a warm environment that appealed to the children. When that point was reached, I believed, problems such as vandalism, poor attendance and unacceptably low achievement rates would virtually vanish. More important, we grew determined to focus on what *could* be done instead of dwelling on things that could *not* be accomplished.

It was not difficult for us to reach agreement on these issues, once the reasons behind them were explained and understood. The ideas I proposed represented substantial change from the way schools habitually function, but they were all focused on creating a sense of happiness and well-being for the children. And as the teachers had been telling me since that first day's visit to South Simcoe, "The children are the reason we are here!" We also agreed that the staff room would become a positive welcoming place, an environment where we would share ideas and feel free to take intellectual risks without fear of criticism, and where "badmouthing" children, parents, other staff members or any aspect of our activities would be banned. Instead, we would share stories of our students' accomplishments and encourage one another whenever we felt discouraged or overwhelmed.

Changes are rarely made in any system without generating discomfort, and that was the case during one of my meetings with the school staff early in my first year at the school. When I proposed moving a classroom from the first floor to the second floor, the teacher angrily—and very loudly—objected. "I have been teaching in that classroom for over twenty years," she said. "And now you come in and tell me you're relocating classrooms and putting me upstairs?"

Someone else added: "You seem to think that moving around classrooms and furniture, and adding a fresh coat of paint here and there, is going to solve the problems. Well, they are not. Do you realize the kinds of things we have to deal with here?"

I was taken aback by the anger of these two teachers. Things had been going well to this point. Later, I realized that adjusting to so many changes in such a short period of time can bring feelings of frustration and bitterness to the surface.

"We have children who come to school hungry because there is no food in the house," said the teacher who objected to having her classroom moved. Her name was Sharon McLean, and I knew she cared about her job and the children with a deep passion. I liked that, even if it meant that I became the target of her frustration and concern. "Or they'll come to school half asleep because their parents were fighting all night long. Or they'll show up here with cuts and bruises from being beaten. I can understand that you want to create a wonderful atmosphere for the children, and we've all agreed on the idea. But that's not enough. How will paint and new classroom locations solve those problems for the kids?"

"They won't," I agreed calmly. "And I'll admit I still have much to learn. But let's think about it. Children who are suffering in that manner need many things, and one of them is a place where they feel welcome, safe and secure. They can even feel loved and cared for here. When they feel all those things, they will be under less emotional stress, and we can do a better job of teaching them. We can build their self-respect and their inner strength, to help them deal with life's challenges and avoid falling into the same kind of life as their parents. If we do that, these kids will become more resilient. That's what I'd like to work towards—together as a team."

I hadn't planned to make a speech, but that's how things turned out, I suppose. More important, I could see more teachers beginning to support my ideas.

"I'm not trying to do this alone," I said. "It can't just be *my* vision. It has to be *our* vision. I need more than your support. I need your ideas and opinions. I need your counsel to tell me what we are doing wrong, and how we can do things better. Most of all, I need your commitment to work with me and make a difference for the kids in this community. Please give me that. If we all agree that the ultimate beneficiaries will be the children, we can afford to be frank with each other."

It worked. Sharon McLean continued to be my harshest critic as well as one of my strongest supporters. The same care and concern she had expressed for the children when she raised her voice at me provided the energy to do what needed to be done, and I will forever thank her for that.

Things were still far from complete on that day in September 1991 when I welcomed the children for the first time as principal. But I could tell from the expressions on their faces that they realized changes had occurred at South Simcoe. Their eyes widened at the sight of the bright posters, plants and curtains, and at the teachers who were turned out smartly in jackets, skirts and slacks.

With school underway, I began tackling some housecleaning chores. I have always believed in surrounding myself with pos-itives—positive people, positive thoughts and positive images—and avoiding reminders of failures. Old school buildings tend to be collection points for discarded materials, and the sight of them carried a message that was exactly oppo-site to what I wanted to convey. I decided that any broken article that could not be restored to its original condition would be dispensed with. There would be no mended furni-ture and no makeshift shelving in South Simcoe. These would become reminders to the staff and students of the past neglect, and I wanted to emphasize the future. I grew determined to find new ways of accessing resources, and I began to lobby hard with board officials on behalf of the school. After all, I reminded myself, when they sent me to South Simcoe, they knew I would rather store books neatly on a clean floor than have them sitting haphazardly on a broken shelf or table.

When we added newly discarded materials to old fur-nishings that had been stored in the basement over the years, the school almost burst at the seams. During the first year I sent twelve truckloads of unwanted objects to the refuse dump or back to the school board office.

Naturally, this "It's good or it's gone" attitude left a few holes in our classroom facilities. But with the clutter gone, we had more room to move about our classrooms. Then, something occurred that convinced me I was meant to be at South Simcoe, and encouraged my determination to find a way to make things better for the children.

Several years earlier, while Ishwar and I were living on campus at the University of Western Ontario, I had made friends with a librarian named Lucy Greene. In fact, Lucy hired me to work in the library with her. By the time I arrived at South Simcoe, Lucy was a senior executive with a giant insurance firm in Toronto, and she was among the first people I called in search of furnishings.

I couldn't believe my luck. Lucy's job and mine fitted together like two pieces of a jigsaw puzzle. Each newly appointed vice-president at Lucy's firm insisted on new furnishings for his or her office. It's a corporate status thing, I suppose. In any case, perfectly good desks, chairs, sofas and computer tables—some only a few years or even a few months old—were constantly being replaced by new furnishings to match new executives' personal taste. Company policy prevented the old furniture from being distributed among its employees, so it sat in limbo, waiting for someone who could use it.

With Lucy's help and her company's generosity, South Simcoe Public School inherited oak credenzas, cozy sofas, comfortable armchairs and a variety of other fine furniture. We added them to the staff room and to a special parents' meeting room, as well as elsewhere in the school. Many of the children (and some of the teachers, we jokingly said) had never curled up in a chair or worked at a desk as comfortable and attractive as the ones they encountered inside the walls of South Simcoe Public School.

Did I call it luck? I believe it was much more than that.

The exterior of the school was more challenging. On Monday mornings we often arrived to discover broken beer bottles on the ground and fresh graffiti on the walls. I have never accepted the idea that these things "just happen" to inner-city schools, and I involved our older students in coming up with a workable solution.

Talking with them, I learned that a supposed "cure" can sometimes make things worse. That was the case, in part, with South Simcoe. In an effort to avoid vandalism, the school sported no lights on its playground at night. The open area continued to attract older children, but there was no outlet for their energies, and the prevailing darkness just seemed to encourage silly pranks.

In response, we installed lights that turned back on whenever anyone was present in the back playground, and added basketball hoops and nets. Our local member of the provincial legislature was so impressed by this single idea that he made a point of stopping by the school and commending us on it.

At this point we made one of those decisions that seemed rather small at the time but proved to be significant in the message it carried. When we asked for basketball equipment, someone at the board office offered hoops and backboards that could be removed and stored inside the school building at the end of each day, to thwart vandalism. We politely refused. The message would be precisely opposite to the one I wanted conveyed to the children and the community. I didn't want anything on or in the school that suggested we didn't trust the kids, or that we didn't want them on the school grounds after hours. To children who wanted to burn off energy in the evenings, with no other recreational facilities nearby, this would have been a slap in the face. So we insisted on installing hoops and nets that remained in place for anyone who wanted to use them.

It worked! Over time, the broken bottles and graffiti decreased, and one morning we arrived to discover the basketball court festooned with a hundred colourful balloons.

"It's a thank-you note," someone said, and I agreed with her totally.

I launched a series of informal chats with senior students at the school to involve them in the changes being made and to enlist their help in accomplishing them. During one of them I casually suggested that the school needed a mascot. They loved the idea, and promised to put their heads together and select one. I assumed they would choose something warm and friendly to reflect the peaceful nature we were trying to create at South Simcoe. You can imagine my horror when the students suggested . . . a shark!

Sharks are mean, cold-blooded predators, I reminded them. They attack and eat people. Who could ever want something as vicious as a shark for a mascot?

"That's the whole idea," one of the students told me. "We want a mean mascot for sports, so we can beat the other team. But he can be a friendly mascot to us." Then he pulled out a pencil and began drawing, with surprising talent, a whole family of friendly sharks, some smiling and winking, and others working.

I was impressed. And convinced. Besides, this wasn't to be my mascot, it was to be the school's, and I had empowered the children to choose it. How could I reject it now?

Once the shark mascot was agreed upon, one of the teachers, Kim Hutchinson, drafted her mother-in-law, Pauline, to depict it throughout the school. We had hired Kim directly out of teachers' college; in addition to being an outstanding teacher, Kim added to the school's success through the sheer power of her enthusiasm.

Pauline is an excellent artist, and within weeks the lower floor of the school had sharks everywhere. Every classroom in the school displayed our shark mascot, and we added the school logo, our motto and a list of our goals. A shark stood with poised pencil and steno pad on the walls of the school office, and a bespectacled shark, painted on the wall of our library, read a book among shark-infested banners that invited students to "Come take a bite out of a book!" Sharks peeked around corners in the downstairs hall, and we even had a shark in the custodian's room—holding a dustpan, of course.

The children were delighted! For some reason kids are fascinated by fearsome creatures like sharks and dinosaurs. Our sharks were as friendly as you would ever want (or *not* want!) to meet, and their presence elevated the level of pride everyone felt in South Simcoe Public School.

Somewhere along the way the staff began referring to me as Mother Bird. I suppose it was in response to the way I kept talking about nurturing our students until they were prepared to fly off to bigger and better things. "If I'm the Mother Bird," I said jokingly one day, "then South Simcoe is my home nest now." The idea of me watching over my "fledglings" really took hold when someone contributed a bottle of Gummy Worms to my office, and the staff began stopping by to nibble them like a flock of hungry baby birds.

The "Mother Bird" nickname launched Pauline on a new round of mural painting. She found some corners of the school that did not sport a shark, and there she displayed nests of baby birds and a mother arriving to feed them. A little room off the library was painted to depict a Victorian

English country garden, with blooming flowers and vines climbing up an elaborate trellis. Joan, our librarian, added lace curtains to the window opening and placed large, comfy cushions on the floor against the wall. It became "The South Simcoe Secret Garden." We knew the younger children would want to curl up there and read books, and they did. But they soon were joined by older children as well, who were drawn to the beauty of this little corner that had sat, dark and empty and unused, for so many years.

The shark proved to be a mascot for the children, but something more was needed to act as a symbol for all that we wanted South Simcoe to represent. I suggested a symbol and a motto that would appear on all official school materials.

We brainstormed with the staff, parents, community members and many of the senior students. We began with the Lamp of Learning, the symbol for all schools in the Durham Region. Lamps provide light, and light leads us through darkness. Then we added hands, to symbolize people reaching out and joining together in partnerships. Soon we had a motto to sum up everything we were working towards at South Simcoe: *Together We Light the Way*.

The words were fine, but we needed a symbol to express them visually. One of our students had boasted about her father's skill as a graphic artist, so I invited the father in to meet with us and discuss designing a school symbol. He listened attentively to our ideas, promised to create the design, and left.

Weeks passed, and we saw nothing of either the father or the symbol design. When I asked the girl what had become of her father and his promise to create a symbol for South Simcoe, her response was, unfortunately, not surprising.

"Dad's been drinking again," she said, disappointed. "But I'll see if I can get him back here."

She must have been persuasive, because the father showed up again, promised to create the design again . . . and vanished again.

This went on for a few weeks, until I realized that some drastic action was needed if South Simcoe were to have its own school symbol before I retired. The next time he arrived, at his daughter's request, I closed the door to my office, handed him a pencil, several sheets of paper and some coloured markers, and said, half-jokingly, that he would not be permitted to leave until he finished his assignment. It made me feel like a primary school teacher again—but it worked. He produced a wonderful symbol for us in purple and yellow, the school colours. I especially liked the way the two hands encircled the lamp of learning, in a gesture that suggested protecting the children.

At the core of my beliefs about education has been the value of *respect*. The value of mutual respect extends beyond the education system, of course, but I have long felt that its role within schools has been underestimated. The key to all that we accomplished at South Simcoe was our focus on respect.

I remembered a childhood lesson from my grandmother. She showed me a bucket of water, the surface of the water as flat and unmarred as a sheet of glass. "You must always be kind and respectful," she told me, "and everything you do must be done with thought and love." Then she poked her index finger into the water. "This is you," she said, indicating her finger. "And this is what happens whenever you do something." She pointed with her other hand at the ripples radiating from her finger, disturbing the water. "It affects other people and everything around you."

I used her lesson to envision respect as the finger she had poked through the surface of the water. The first circle represented yourself. The circles radiating out from it represented, in order, your schoolmates, friends, teachers, family and the community. When you respect people, you treat them with kindness. You encourage them. You treat them with the same respect you yourself want to receive.

As the circles widen, they reach beyond the people and places around us to include global issues. You respect other cultures, other races and both genders. You avoid racism and sexism, just as you avoid polluting the environment, and you refuse to ridicule the handicapped. All of these attitudes are based on respect, and all true respect begins by respecting yourself.

Our Respect program applied these principles to everything we did at South Simcoe. When asked, "How did you people manage to achieve so much in that school?" we referred the questioner to the Respect program. The answer was there.

Keeping a school clean and tidy is always a challenge, and in spite of the transformation we were making, it remained a concern at South Simcoe. In a meeting I held with Gail and Randy, the custodians, Gail explained that she was allotted only half an hour to clean each room. Most of that time, she informed me, was spent removing pencils, pieces of erasers, crumpled papers and other discarded materials from the floor, where they had been tossed by students. "That doesn't leave me much time for dusting and cleaning," she said.

I asked if she had any suggestions for solving the problem.

Gail noted that, while we were emphasizing teamwork in the school, it didn't seem to be applied to helping the custodial staff—and she was right. "If we can just get the kids to see it from my point of view, maybe they would understand how they are making things difficult for me," she said.

I thought this was a fine idea and invited her to explain things to one of the senior classes. It seemed to me that the children should assume some responsibility for their school's cleanliness.

The next day, in the classroom, Gail entered with a vacuum cleaner and dramatically emptied its contents onto the floor in front of the students. "This is what I picked up from your room yesterday," she told them. She could have picked up even more, she explained, but some items kept clogging her vacuum. "I can't clean your classroom as well as I should because I spend so much of my time picking things off the floor that you could be putting in the wastebasket or storing away in your cupboards and desks."

The children were aghast. They had had no idea of the extra work they were creating for Gail, or perhaps no one had taken the time to explain her duties in this way. Whatever the reason, they immediately began apologizing for the extra work they were creating for an already overworked woman, and began putting their heads together to find a solution.

"How about a fifteen-minute cleanup session at the end of every day?" somebody suggested, and the children agreed. Eventually, the idea was adopted by the entire school, expressing not only the ability of the kids to solve a problem, but also demonstrate their respect for others.

And it didn't stop there. A week later the two custodians came up with a method of recognizing the children's efforts in the school. Each Friday, Gail and Randy selected the cleanest classroom for that week and presented them with the Golden Dustpan Award to be displayed proudly. The custodians purchased a dustpan, covered it with gold paint and added a drawing of our shark mascot to it. Every classroom in the school vied to win at least once during the school year. As a result we not only had a cleaner school but two smiling custodians as well.

We also, I hasten to add, had a smarter principal, who realized she could learn a great deal by listening carefully to the staff and involving others in developing effective solutions.

One day I received a telephone call from a warm and gracious man named Carl Reimer. Carl, a member of the local Kiwanis Club, had heard of our accomplishments from a social worker and believed in the things we were doing. "You're on the right track," he assured us, and asked how he and other members of his club could help as partners.

I suggested that Carl could read to our younger students and chat with our older children on Monday afternoons, and he did so with such enthusiasm that the children quickly warmed to him. In fact, Mondays became Carl Reimer days at the school, shining and warm with his grandfatherly presence as he enthralled the younger children by reading stories aloud in his mellow voice. Older students grew to trust Carl as a "Dutch Uncle," a man to whom they could vent their frustration and always receive a sympathetic hearing.

I began referring to Carl as my Guardian Angel, because he arrived just when we needed someone like him—an understanding and compassionate man who said, simply: "I want to help you." Over time, we learned to consult Carl about new ideas. We would brainstorm them with Carl and bounce suggestions off him to help decide which concepts were practical and which needed more planning. We valued his wisdom and opinions, especially because he expressed them according to our standard, which was *What's best for our children?*

Carl submitted ideas of his own, and when he proposed holding a weekend bicycle rodeo for the children, we agreed it was a good one. He suggested holding the rodeo at the school. We would start early on a Saturday morning and the children would learn the importance of wearing a safety helmet, how to check their bikes for safety and how to negotiate an obstacle course. As icing on the cake, Carl's Kiwanis Club would donate a brand-new bicycle, to be won in a raffle.

I loved the idea, but I had to agree with some of Sharon McLean's concerns. Friday night was Party Night in the South Simcoe area, and many of the children might have difficulty arriving for an early start on Saturday morning—not to mention the adult volunteers. We had never held an event like this in the school, which made the response of the children unpredictable. What if no one showed up? What if it rained? What if . . . ?

We ran the gamut of what-ifs and decided to hold the First Annual South Simcoe Bike Rodeo in spite of so many misgivings. Even if just twenty people showed up early Saturday morning, I pointed out, we could consider the event a success; so let's do it. With Sharon's realistic cautions in mind, we went ahead with organizing the event, and I went home on Friday evening looking forward to it.

When I woke up early the next morning and looked out my bedroom window, I saw . . . rain. Steady, depressing, drizzly rain falling from a low, grey sky. As I dressed and prepared to drive to the school, I refused to accept the possibility of being defeated by bad weather, and I began willing the rain away.

The rain was still falling when I arrived at the school about eight o'clock and found a series of puddles and a half-dozen soggy community partners waiting for me. "I'm willing the sun to arrive!" I announced, which generated some uncertain smiles from Carl and the others.

Things got better almost immediately. The rain became a light mist and soon ceased completely. The small group grew steadily with the improving weather until, by ten-thirty, about a hundred kids, Kiwanis Club members and parent volunteers were on hand. Soon the sun was shining in all its warmth, the puddles were vanishing, the children were learning important safety rules, and the Kiwanis members were fulfilling their mandate of providing important services to the community.

I had brought the sun to South Simcoe with the sheer force of my will and my determination that nothing would spoil the day for the kids. Doubt it if you will, but I remain convinced anyway.

Lessons for all of us were acquired in various ways at South Simcoe. When I learned from a parent whose mother had attended the school that South Simcoe had once boasted lovely rose gardens along the south wall, we decided to restore the grounds to their original splendour. That spring Jacki Devolin, one of our teaching assistants, recruited a team of students to canvass the neighbourhood for volunteers, garden tools and bedding plants. Many of the people they approached were pleasantly surprised to learn we were not looking for money. We didn't want their money—we wanted their support and involvement as a community. Nor would their contributions benefit the school exclusively. In fact, since the flowers would be planted just prior to the school's closing for summer vacation, the neighbourhood would enjoy their beauty as much as anyone at the school. Sharon proposed planting flowers in front of the nearby Legion Hall as well, which by this time had provided us with extra facilities.

We had another, more subtle motive behind our gardening efforts. We wanted to demonstrate how many things of little or no value to others—including used and often broken garden tools, rejected spindly plants, and even the long-ignored grounds surrounding the school—could be put to good use with a little care, time and effort.

Not even the heavy rain that fell on our first Community Day could dampen the enthusiasm of our planting team. Included on the team were Ruth, our school trustee; Doug, our librarian; two local business people; and a large team of teachers and students. They all cut armholes in plastic garbage bags, slid them on as waterproof vests, tied others around their heads as hats, and set to work.

Once again we discovered we had set something in motion that was much larger than anticipated. We all took turns watering the flowers during the summer, but more than our periodic efforts were necessary to keep the flowers blooming. Two employees of the Kmart store in the plaza across the street began eating lunch beneath the tree in our garden. When they noticed the flowers were wilting from the heat, they borrowed a sprinkling can from the store's display and watered them thoroughly.

Our second Community Day included a fun fair on the playground, complete with ponies who, with delighted children on their backs, were led around the grounds by two staff members. Inside the school, invited guests munched on cookies and sandwiches, entertained by songs and presentations from each class.

From there, Community Day seemed to acquire a life of its own. In the following years members of our planting team included the mayor, various politicians, school board members, mascots from local businesses, several police officers and firefighters, and so many other volunteers that we were running short of room to plant the flowers. Many Grade Eight students, who were on their way to high school, offered to tend the flowers during summer vacation.

Community Day activities eventually moved inside the school when our community partners began touring the classes. We wanted the partners to experience the difference they were making to the children and their education. We also, of course, relished the opportunity for the children to show off their achievements.

In every classroom, students placed their *Together We Light the Way* portfolios on their desks, prepared to discuss their accomplishments one-on-one with their visitors. These accomplishments were wide-ranging and invariably impressive to the partners—not just because of the way the children described the good choices they had made and the goals they had achieved, but the manner in which they supported their stories with graphs to trace their progress in reading, mathematics and other areas.

We learned several lessons from Community Day. We discovered that everyone wants to be part of a success, and once the success of our event became apparent, there was no need to reach out for workers and supplies—we often were offered more than we could handle.

Community Day also taught a lesson to the small handful of skeptics. "The school planted flowers there before," they said when we first proposed the idea, "and vandals always ripped them out."

None of the flowers from Community Day suffered from vandalism. Why? Because "the school" hadn't planted them. They had been planted by the entire community, including the students, the staff and the mayor, plus police officers, firefighters, business people, mascots and service club members. And the community assumed ownership of the garden.

Other lessons were acquired from the garden as well, including some we neither wanted nor anticipated.

When an overenthusiastic student knocked a branch from one of the young trees planted on our grounds one day, he used it as a weapon, chasing others across the play area. They in turn ripped more branches from the tree, and before Cathie, one of the supervising teachers, could bring a halt to the mayhem, ten branches had been torn from the little tree.

Cathie carried them in her arms to my office, her eyes welling up. "Look what they did, Sandra," she said. "Look what the kids did."

I couldn't believe it. "Not our kids?" I said.

"Yes," she said, "*our* kids."

"Tell me they're all new to our school," I almost pleaded. South Simcoe kids didn't go around destroying property. They respected their school and the environment, and this kind of thing went against everything we were striving to teach them. These must have been new students who hadn't yet tuned in to our program.

"They're not new," she said. "They just got carried away."

I rarely became angry, but this one struck a nerve. "I

need to see them all," I instructed Cathy. It meant removing children from class, something I rarely did. It was an expression, I suppose, of my disappointment.

With all the students gathered in my office, looking sheepish and, I admit, a little anxious, I displayed the branches to them. "How could this happen?" I asked. "How could our students, students of this school, do such a thing? How could children such as you, who take pride in our school and our gardens, do such damage? Please explain this to me."

They blurted out a series of explanations. "We were just fooling around." "We got carried away." "We didn't mean to."

I could see they were truly sorry. But I also saw an opportunity to teach an important lesson. Children, I knew, can seem to be destructive when they are simply being thoughtless.

"Do you realize you severely injured a living thing?" I asked them. They hadn't considered things in that light before. "A tree has life," I said. "A different kind of life from your own, but it's still a life." I held the branches up for them to see. "This is what you did to a living thing." Then I set the branches on a table in my office and sat staring at them, as though I were mourning them, while the children found their way back to their classes.

The next day I carried the branches in my arms from class to class and explained what had happened to them. I didn't name the children responsible for the damage, because I didn't want revenge or punishment; I wanted them to understand the seriousness of the matter. I explained how sad it made me and the other teachers, how the torn branches had damaged our environment, and how such damage was not what we expected from our school and our students. Then I asked for suggestions to ensure this never happened again.

The students took this lesson very seriously. Some even proposed that anyone who went closer than ten feet to a tree should be suspended. We did not go that far, of course. The point had been made, and the lesson had been learned.

Our care for the garden reflected our care for the children who attended the school, and it generated so much beauty that South Simcoe Public School won the 1995 Looking Good Award as the most attractive of all 120 elementary schools within the board's jurisdiction.

Changes to the school's inner and outer appearance were making an impact, no doubt. This was a key goal, because it began to build pride and ownership in the school by the students and the community. But the major challenge, I knew, was to make changes within the students themselves, and this involved more than exterior appearance.

It meant touching their hearts and minds.

Chapter 4
. . . . . .

Loss and Renewal

*I*t is true that the more you give love, the more you receive it in return. But the loss of something, or someone, you love is never diluted as a result. The unexpected loss I suffered during that first year at South Simcoe was no less painful and searing just because I was learning to love the school, the staff, the children and my work. In some ways, these made it more agonizing.

I had come to South Simcoe Public School with many hopes and expectations, but with very few answers. In fact, I learned that there is never a single answer or set of answers when dealing with the challenges facing the children of areas such as South Simcoe. We had to create our own solutions by working together among ourselves and with our community partners.

During September of my first year at South Simcoe, two Grade Eight boys raced down the hall towards my office, followed by several other worried students. I heard them coming, shouting as they ran: "Where's the principal? Where's the principal?"

"What's the problem?" I asked when I emerged to discover what was going on.

"A man in a truck tried to take away two of our girls!" they said.

The abduction of a student is a nightmarish fear faced by teachers and parents alike. I asked where the girls were, trying to conceal my apprehension.

"We have them," one boy said, and the other added, "They're only six years old."

The girls had been walking home through the mall opposite the school when a man drove up in a van and offered them some candy. When they approached to take it from his hand, he tried to pull them inside. The two Grade Eight boys, witnessing the attempted abduction, rushed to the vehicle and pulled the girls away. The boys also alertly recorded the van's licence number, proving that despite—or because of—the challenges confronting many children at South Simcoe, they were very streetwise.

Two detectives arrived in response to my telephone call and interviewed me, the Grade Eight boys and the little girls who had almost been abducted. When they completed the interviews and began to leave, one of the girls tugged at my skirt. "Ask for their badge numbers," she said, indicating the officers.

I was a little confused, and asked why it was important.

"In case you need more information," she replied.

Even the detectives were impressed. "She's right," one of them said. "You need both an incident number and a badge number. That way, we can bring you up to date on the progress of things."

After the police left, I looked down at this little waiflike beauty who, just an hour or so before, had narrowly missed being abducted in broad daylight by a repulsive pervert. "Are you all right?" I asked.

She smiled as though to reassure me, the adult and professional educator. "Yes, I'm fine," she said. Then she asked if I was all right, and advised me not to worry. With the excitement behind her, and confident that I had survived the event as well as she had, she skipped down the hall as though she didn't have a worry in the world.

Me? I remained frazzled for the rest of the day.

We were continually being surprised by the street-smart character and maturity of the students at South Simcoe. One day a member of our staff, a bright young teacher named Doug Beeston, was reading to a kindergarten class. They remained quiet and attentive until Doug came to a passage in the book that referred to babies springing from cabbage patches. Suddenly the entire class shot their hands up in the air. "That's not where they come from!" the children protested, and before Doug could respond, one boy began reciting the process of procreation in exquisite and colourful detail while all the other children nodded soberly in agreement.

The children were calm about the event, but Doug was still flustered when he described the incident to me later that day. "I just wanted to read them a story," he said. "I didn't want to teach a sex-education class to a bunch of five year olds."

I assured him we all had much to learn from our street-wise student body.

Other events faced by the staff were not quite as humorous, and often more dramatic. One day early in September, Andrea, a Grade Eight teacher, was covering a class for another member of staff, who had become ill. We had managed to obtain a supply teacher, but unfortunately she was not equipped to deal with some of the behaviour encountered at South Simcoe and, halfway through her teaching day, she threw up her hands and fled the school. This left me with no one except Andrea, a new teacher, to supervise the class. Upon entering the room, Andrea discovered one of the students, an extremely bright girl, barking like a dog. The girl had removed her shoes and stockings and placed wads of tissues between her toes. While this was happening, another young student was performing somersaults across the desks, risking broken bones or worse, and a third announced that Andrea was not to speak directly to her but to her stuffed toy mouse.

Andrea said it was like entering a setting for a *Twilight Zone* episode. The total pandemonium in the class was in sharp contrast with everything we were trying to achieve at South Simcoe. Fortunately, Andrea was able to deal with the situation by applying techniques we had developed together.

She knew that the girl who was barking like a dog suffered from a multiple personality disorder, and was awaiting placement in a high-care facility. The student who insisted on the teacher talking not to her but to her "pet mouse" was undergoing serious psychological trauma. Andrea remained calm and applied a number of strategies we used in the school to redirect behaviour. One was the use of "safe places" for angry children. A safe place was an agreed-upon location, such as my office or the library, where a student could withdraw until his or her anger subsided. An older child could even, under special circumstances, leave the school and calm down alone on the playground, if that proved more effective.

Often, it seemed as though each time we solved a problem or overcame an obstacle, another appeared to take its place. How could we possibly keep up with this volume of new (and sometimes reappearing) challenges? The answer was a special staff, of course—and special staff meetings.

By getting together as a staff to share ideas and experiences, we were able to identify strategies that helped the students, and eventually refine them for even more effectiveness. So instead of traditional monthly meetings, we scheduled them every two weeks.

More meetings were fine, but they placed extra stress on the staff, whose time was already stretched. To honour and respect the fact that everyone had commitments beyond the school, we agreed to keep the length of the meetings to just one hour.

How did we manage to fit so many concerns, and enable so many people to express their views, in just one hour? In a word: *organization*. We all worked to make the meetings informative and fun, even while we were working hard to develop solutions, discuss issues and share ideas. For example, every session began with music, and featured snacks and treats to enjoy.

More important, we insisted on focusing on positive results. We kept asking, "What worked well?" and "What can we do to make it even more effective?" Everyone who attended our meetings grew assured that their opinions were valued and their ideas would be given serious consideration. This did more than generate effective ideas—it also gave everyone a true sense of partnership in the running of the school. We became a large, cohesive team, sharing leadership and all committed to making our ideas effective and attaining our goals.

During my first year at South Simcoe it quickly became apparent that the most immediate goal academically was teaching the children to read. When I had taught Grade

One, my goal had been to have my students reading by the end of the school year. Yet, during that first year at South Simcoe, we had large numbers of students unable to read in Grade Five.

This was a reflection of the reality of the South Simcoe community, the transient nature of many families there, and the social and economic difficulties faced by both the parents and children. When students are being distracted by major problems at home—problems ranging from hunger to severe physical and mental abuse—the intense concentration required for reading simply vanishes.

Working with trustee Ruth Lafarga, we set ourselves the goal of every South Simcoe student reading by Grade Five. We knew that our goal-setting plan would prove to be an empty gesture without the wholehearted support and involvement of the parents. To involve them, we made use of weekly tracking sheets, sent home with every student to inform parents of the progress being made in their child's weekly program—sort of a customized weekly report card. All students received weekly tracking sheets, and those needing higher levels of help took a tracking sheet home with them daily. The tracking sheets noted the goals set by the child and teacher together each morning, and the progress made by the end of the day. Two questions on the daily tracking sheets were asked and answered: What have I done well today? and, What do I need to focus on tomorrow? The teacher sometimes added comments and personal notes.

The tracking sheets served several purposes. First, they represented a medium of communication with parents. Also, since we asked the parents to use the tracking sheets by making comments on them before signing and having the students return them, the children learned that we cared about the parents' opinions, and that the parents cared about the school's opinions. Finally, the sheets prevented surprises at report-card time.

Perfecting the knack of using the tracking sheets took a great deal of time at first. We introduced the system with just one class the first year, working out the details and refining the system. Then we added three more classes in the second year, and by the third year tracking sheets were being used throughout the school. A team approach was necessary, and it worked—usually. From time to time Sharon McLean might say that we were moving too fast, that our goals were too lofty and that my expectations were too high. "Sandra," I heard more than once, "we need to slow down a bit and catch our breath!"

Comments like these would cause me to reassess the speed of our program introductions, and they also encouraged an honest exchange among everyone. We would talk about the difficulties being encountered, discuss alternatives and invariably reach a solution to benefit everyone. In many ways, the disagreements and their resolution actually strengthened our teamwork.

Inevitably, regrettable incidents occurred. Once, I suggested to a veteran male teacher that some simple adjustments to his report cards might make them easier for the parents of his students to understand. He responded by swearing at me in front of a group of parents and students who happened to be passing in the main hallway. I put on a brave face, but I admit I drove home in tears.

Later I set up a meeting with this same teacher, where we began to resolve our differences, and I learned that timing is everything. Many things were falling into place. Progress was being made. Our goals, which had once seemed overly ambitious and unattainable, now were being achieved. Christmas was coming, and we were all looking forward to sharing our success amid the joy the holiday season has always meant to me. It would also bring, of course, a much-needed break for the staff.

Then, on the very afternoon that the male teacher agreed to redo his report cards and we shook hands, vowing to work together on behalf of the kids, my brother called from Trinidad to inform me that my father had died. The words came to me through a blur of emotion and gloom. A heart attack. No warning. Sixty-six years old, much too young. Funeral plans. Family gathering.

The death of a parent is traumatic for everyone, and I do not intend to suggest that I suffered any more pain or sadness than someone else in my position. But everything seemed so *unfair*. Here I was, determined to improve the lives of children, creating a team of wonderfully dedicated professionals, demonstrating all the beliefs I had held through so much of my life and teaching career . . . and I had been so busy that I couldn't remember the last time I had told my father I loved him. What did all my achievements mean now?

They meant as much as ever, of course. I knew that in my heart. But as the eldest child in our family I had enjoyed a special relationship with my father. When I was a small child, he would rock me gently on his knee and read to me from storybooks. He taught me how to draw flowers, and he had a special way of whistling my name as I arrived home from school. He told me I was the most special girl in the world and that I could become any person I wanted to be.

Naturally, I believed him, and that belief is at the core of who and what I am today.

I know that millions of parents express the same kind of love and support to their children each day, and their children are blessed because of it. But this was *my* father saying these things to *me*, and despite what my mind knew, my heart had always believed he would live forever. Now he was gone, without even a goodbye spoken between us. He was the first close relative I lost to death, and to say I was devastated as I replaced the receiver after that telephone call . . . well, there is no word to describe my emotion.

With encouragement from colleagues at the board office, two teachers were designated to assume my duties, working closely with my secretary, Joan Strzelczyk. Then I set off for my sad journey to Trinidad.

The days I spent there are now a jumble of memories— tears, hugs, stories of my father's kindnesses, and a reaffirmation of all that my family meant to me. I returned to Canada during the Christmas vacation with a strange longing simply to stay at home. As much as I loved the kids, and the challenge I had accepted at South Simcoe, I was emotionally drained and unable to find the energy to continue dealing with the stress and struggle involved in realizing my vision for the school.

Let's face it, I discovered myself thinking one day, you are an inexperienced principal dealing with some very experienced staff members, and you are trying to make a lot of changes without alienating those around you. You may believe in what you are doing, but until everyone around you believes in it the same way, with the same dedication, you aren't going to achieve your goal. Accept that it will be a long, slow and often painful process. And eventually I did.

Some obstacles at the school that seemed overwhelming had nothing to do with the staff. In spite of assistance from surprising sources, such as my friend at the insurance company, the school still needed essential items like good bulletin boards and carpeting. The delays in obtaining furnishings and materials, and the tight restrictions on expenditures, were doubly frustrating because we were starting to see the rewards of our efforts.

I knew that other school officials were facing the same challenge of limited funds and equipment, but it seemed doubly unfair to us at South Simcoe. In my emotional state I seriously questioned whether I could maintain the confidence I had shown to others—a confidence I felt eroding within me after my father died. I simply did not want to return to South Simcoe. I wanted only to stay home, where I felt safe and warm and loved.

That's when another of those events that others call "luck" occurred. I prefer to think of it as proof of the Eastern proverb: *When the student is ready, the teacher will appear.*

About a week before school resumed, at the very height of my self-doubts, I began to express my uncertainties to a friend, Phyliss. Another woman, Hyacinth, happened to be visiting my friend's house, overheard us and suggested I speak to a man she knew named Steve Ramsanker. Steve had just been awarded the Order of Canada for his work at the Alex Taylor Community School in Edmonton, a school that had been facing many of the same challenges as South Simcoe. Like me, Steve was from Trinidad, which made it easier for me to talk with him by telephone.

As I spoke to Steve, I felt my doubts begin to fade and my resolve return. Part of it was the familiar island lilt in his voice, and part of it was his enormous energy and infectious sense of humour. "I'm a Rhodes scholar," he says to most people when meeting them for the first time. Then, giving them a sly look, he adds: "The railroads." After immigrating to Canada, Steve had paid for his college education by working on the railway in western Canada.

It was Steve's description of his experiences at Alex Taylor Community School, however, that I most wanted to hear. The school is in Edmonton's toughest neighbourhood, set among taverns and cut-rate hotels, where students have to thread their way among prostitutes and drug dealers on their way to and from classes. The annual murder rate in the compact Alex Taylor neighbourhood often equalled the rate in all the neighbourhoods of the rest of the city combined.

Many of Steve's educational philosophies were remarkably similar to the ones I envisioned for South Simcoe, but Steve had gone even farther. To alleviate the hunger of children who often arrived at school without breakfast, Steve served them early-morning meals of moose-meat cakes and fried bannock, as well as more traditional fare, often paid for out of his own pocket.

Food wasn't the only need faced by these children. Many wore tattered, dirty clothing, so Steve actually convinced the board to install showers, a washing machine and a clothes dryer in the school for students to use to keep themselves clean and neat. The improvement in the sense of self-worth among these children was enormous, and naturally, it affected their attitude towards school and learning.

Steve's dedication to his work and his students was nothing less than awe-inspiring. He wanted the students at Alex Taylor to realize that another world existed beyond their inner-city neighbourhood. On three occasions he took students to his native Trinidad to experience the culture and values there—once mortgaging his house to cover the expenses. During his stint at Alex Taylor, he had arranged for over 2,500 students and 400 seniors to travel across Canada and the United States, and into the Caribbean. As word of his achievements spread, Steve was often tempted away from Alex Taylor by offers from government and university groups, but he stubbornly remained where he was. "This is the special mission I was born to," he would say, sounding very much like my grandmother.

When I expressed the misgivings I had been feeling, Steve's response was: "The path you have chosen is not an easy one. You will have to draw on all the strength you have inside, and reach beyond yourself to give the children what they need." I must have expressed at least a little doubt, because he added: "You can do it. You *will* do it. I'll be here to support you. Call me anytime you need me."*

Steve's inspiring words were like a tonic to me. I resolved to continue pursuing our goals at South Simcoe, discarding any idea of giving up in favour of reading in a cozy chair at home every day.

I returned to the school a changed person in many ways. Staff members tell me I became more patient, more willing to accept that we could not change everything overnight. I'm told that I also became more approachable after my father's death and after hearing Steve's words. At the time I was unaware of any change. Now, on reflection, I think the

---

* Later in my first year at South Simcoe, another principal and I arranged for Steve to travel from Edmonton and address the staffs at our two schools. He emphasized the need for all staff members to offer their total support and total involvement, and praised the concept of schools reaching out to the community. The audience was moved by his words. Steve was able to touch them in a way that energized them to continue their work.

passing of my father strengthened his lessons of tolerance in me, along with the realization that I could not achieve all that I wanted to achieve on my own. I could envision, I could lead, I could encourage and I could participate. But I could not change all that needed changing by myself, like some warrior riding alone to do battle with injustice. That was comic-book fantasy. At South Simcoe, we dealt with real-world challenges every day, and I needed a strong team to work together with me.

An example of a real-world challenge came with the arrival of Desmond Harris*, an angry Grade Eight student who was constantly bullying other children, including his own younger brother. We tried a variety of strategies. Our attempt to involve his parents in the process proved fruitless; in their eyes, Desmond was "just being a boy," and they did nothing to support our efforts.

Desmond's problems became a nightmare during a visit by his class to the Royal Ontario Museum in Toronto, where Desmond seriously damaged an exhibit before running off to hide in a washroom. When the teachers were unable to locate him, the class tour was cancelled, disappointing dozens of students. Museum officials also stated, in no uncertain terms, that Desmond would not be welcomed back.

Around the same time, we discovered that Desmond had been bullying several younger students, stealing their lunch money and using it to purchase pizza for himself. This was totally unacceptable, so I suspended him. I did this with some regret, because suspensions are a last resort and

---

*   I have used pseudonyms for students and their families throughout the book.

never a true solution. What's more, in spite of the boy's actions, I sensed a goodness within him. That's not the opinion of some idealistic dreamer, by the way. I had talked to Desmond and watched him respond to my words. You could reason with him, and for a time he would become the most wonderful child, before sliding back into his role as an angry, resentful bully.

What I remember most fondly about Desmond was his voice. He sang in the school choir, and frequently took solos. When he did, the sound of his voice could bring tears to your eyes, and suddenly he was no longer a bully but a specially gifted child. I need to make this point because it is too easy to measure a child's worth according to only one or two dimensions. Yes, Desmond was aggressive and hostile, but he was as complex as any human being; and the special qualities within him justified all the effort we expended on him. Unfortunately, it came to naught, with disturbing consequences for me.

Nothing else had motivated Desmond's parents to become actively involved in changing his attitude, but our decision to suspend him generated an immediate hostile reaction.

Desmond's father arrived at my office the following day, furious at me for suspending his son. He was a large man who towered over me, and my staff and I had encountered him on earlier occasions during discussions about Desmond's progress and attitude. The man's very presence was intimidating, especially to women, whom he ogled as though undressing them with his eyes. He always tried to arrange meetings with the female staff after 5 P.M., when he knew the custodians had left for the day and he could intimidate them further.

Now his anger exploded into screams and threats, all of them directed at me, and my explanations only seemed to fuel his hostility. I had to stand my ground. Staff and students, I knew, were aware of our encounter. They could hear Desmond's father ranting and raving, thumping the desk and shouting abuse at me, acting in the same manner that we had been telling students was unacceptable from them. How, then, could it be acceptable from this man? I refused to lift the suspension on Desmond, and the father finally left my office, but not without spewing threats against me, the school, the school board and much of the universe.

One morning he stormed past my secretary and some children gathered around her, entering my office with his fist raised, already shouting curses and threats.

"You bitch!" he roared, slamming the door shut behind him. "I'm going to deal with you!"

I sat at my desk, petrified.

"I'm fed up with you," he said before I could speak. "I'm sick of you picking on my boy, picking on my family, picking on me!"

I managed to remain outwardly calm. Then, remembering he was a classic bully, I stood up and made my way around my desk. He remained between me and the door. "Get out of my way!" I said in my loudest voice.

My authoritative manner obviously caught him off guard, because he reacted by stepping aside.

"Call the police," I said to Joan when I opened the door. "This man is bullying and threatening me." Wide-eyed, she reached for the telephone. Children who had witnessed the man's actions and overheard his angry shouts watched with concern, and one six-year-old girl burst into tears, running to me and hugging me, asking if I was all right.

I assured her I was fine just as the man strode out of my office, subdued a little by my instruction to call the police. "Don't think this is the end of this," he said, pointing his finger at me. "You just watch!"

Desmond's father was unemployed, and whether this was the cause or the effect of his rage was unclear. It didn't matter. His fury grew white-hot, all of it aimed at me. He even visited the director at the board office, sweeping documents from her desk onto the floor in an explosion of rage before leaving. He also tried to contact the minister of education, which got him nowhere.

Unable to find support from official sources, he launched into an even more bitter personal attack on me. Soon, letters began arriving, calling me a bitch, a tyrant, and using other unspeakable words to express his opinion of me. He placed copies of his letters under the windshields of cars in our parking lot and in the mall across the street. That day, I drove home in tears. Once again I began questioning my decisions, my resolve.

One parent, familiar with Desmond's father and his actions, advised me to back down. "He's a bully," she said. "He won't give you a moment's peace. Why not just drop the whole thing and get on with your life? It's not the end of the world."

Perhaps she was right. I could back down and give in to his threats. After all, I had expected hurdles when I accepted the position, but not character assassination or the threat of physical violence. Besides, I hadn't suspended Desmond in a moment of spite or weakness. It had been a carefully considered decision, taken as a last resort to demonstrate that we could not accept his behaviour, and to ensure the other students that South Simcoe was a safe haven for them.

My husband, Ishwar, provided a solid foundation of support, as usual. "Do what you think is right," he advised. "Do what you can live with, and what you can tell our children about without being shamed or embarrassed."

For a very long time, I sat quietly reassessing everything I had done, and all the difficulties it had created. The truth is, I seriously considered backing away from the issue. Was the parent justified in his anger at me? Had I done the correct thing after all? Should I back down and resolve the matter, or continue to fight, making things more difficult for everyone on my staff and at the board office?

I went back and forth with these questions all evening, until I accepted one clear realization: The man was a bully, no more and no less. We had begun helping the children to deal with bullies and violence on the playground, teaching them ways to prevent bullying and thus its harmful effects. How, then, could I simply walk away from this bullying situation, just because it affected me directly? What kind of message would that deliver to the children?

I finally went to bed, knowing the answer.

A few days later I invited the staff to a meeting at our house to discuss the situation and my decision. The staff was already aware of all the details when I explained that I would not back down to threats and abuse from Desmond's father. I welcomed their opinions, then asked for their support, warning them that they might become targets of his abuse themselves. "He may say things about me directly to you," I explained, "and if you defend me in any way, he could turn his anger on you. So this is a decision that will affect everyone in this room, and I cannot make it in peace unless I know I have your total support."

I got it. The staff, bless their hearts, backed me one

hundred percent, and at the end of the meeting we were, all of us, closer and more dedicated than ever. This was the first time I spoke to them so openly about my personal feelings, and I realized how much like a family we were becoming.

The harassment continued, and Desmond's father grew even more irate. When he started waiting for me in the parking lot, prepared to scream abuse at me at the end of the school day, staff and parents began escorting me to my car. We complained to the police, of course, and obtained a court order warning him against trespassing in the school, but with little effect. He continued to lurk, sometimes hanging around the schoolyard, sometimes boldly entering the building and walking out again just to prove we were unable to banish him. And so it went, through the balance of the school year.

But something good came of this. Parents began thanking me for taking a stand against him. Many of them were the man's neighbours and were familiar with his bullying tactics. Their support for me extended to offering stronger support for the school. By standing up for my beliefs, I taught a lesson to the children and earned the respect and appreciation of their parents. Together with the bonding that resulted from the meeting with staff at my home, it built us all into a tighter, more cohesive group, prepared to do whatever was necessary to make South Simcoe the kind of school we all wanted it to be. That's the ironic result of this entire episode, as painful and disturbing as it was.

At year's end, when Desmond completed Grade Eight and went on to high school, his father gave up. A twinge of sadness runs through my memory when I recall this. As I mentioned earlier, at heart Desmond was a decent kid. We built a stronger team at the school as a result of his father's outrageous actions, it's true. But although there appears to have been no alternative to our actions, I feel we somehow failed Desmond. And I still miss hearing his sweet voice singing in the choir.

My dreadful experience with Desmond and his father was balanced by several smaller, less dramatic but no less important episodes. All of them taught us things about the children and their needs. Many involved children like Janice, whose need was so basic we almost overlooked it.

Janice was a Grade Seven student with learning problems. She had failed earlier grades, leaving her well behind her friends, who would be advancing to high school the following year while Janice remained at South Simcoe. Peer status, of course, is important to children in their early teens, and Janice's was about to suffer a blow she did not feel capable of handling. Her social worker, who was trying to guide and encourage Janice, alerted us that Janice was planning to drop out. "I want to go to high school with my friends," Janice tearfully confessed to her. "If I can't go to high school, I'll quit. I'm too old to be hanging around with the kids at South Simcoe for another year."

Thanks to the attention she was receiving at South Simcoe, Janice was making great progress. None of us wanted to see her toss away her best chance to obtain an education, even though we understood her frustration and her embarrassment at past failures.

Refusing to write Janice off—you never write children off, in my opinion—I invited her to my office for a chat, and asked Jacki, who was especially fond of Janice, to sit in.

"Is it true you're thinking of leaving school?" I asked Janice when we were settled.

She nodded glumly, avoiding my eyes.

"I don't understand why you would think of doing such a thing," I said. "Especially now, when you seem to be doing so well. We're proud of what you are doing. Aren't you proud of it?"

"I guess so," Janice said. She looked so forlorn and confused. Her eyes began to fill with tears. "I just want to be with my friends more than I want to be here."

"Everyone wants to be with friends," I said. "But your education is important too. You have been working hard, and your teachers have worked hard to help you, Janice. You're beginning to make great improvement. Don't you care about it? Because we do."

She looked directly at me for the first time, with an expression of hope and maybe surprise.

"We do, Janice," I assured her. "We care about you. All of us." Then I added: "And we love you, Janice. We care about you and love you. Can't you see that?"

"You never said that before," she said. "You never said that you cared about me or loved me."

"Janice, you know I love you," Jacki said. I had never seen such relief and gratitude in a child's eyes as I saw when Janice heard those words. "We all do, and we want what's best for you. We want you to stay in school."

"I needed to hear you say that," Janice said. Then she smiled, her eyes glistening with tears. "OK," she said. "I'll stay."

Jacki and I were stunned. That was all it took? All we had to do was tell Janice was that we cared about her and loved her?

It was true. Janice stayed, completed Grade Seven, excelled in Grade Eight and went on to high school. We made no threats or pleas, and we painted no glum pictures of a life ruined without an education. That wasn't what

Janice needed. She simply needed us to tell her we cared, and that we loved her.

Once again a student had taught the teachers. It wasn't enough for us to provide academic instruction; we also needed to provide a foundation of love and support.

After the meeting with Janice, I began to apply the lesson over and over again. In fact, just a few days later, one of the teachers began describing her troubles with a particular student who just didn't seem to care about school, about life, about anything.

"He needs to know you care about him," I advised the teacher.

"But I do," she replied.

"Then tell him," I said. "Let him hear it. Believe me, I've seen it work. And I think it's a good idea, once a day, to tell all the children in your class that you care about them. If you're not comfortable about saying it to the entire class, then say it to one child a day. But *say* it."

It never failed to work with children who craved the comfort of knowing that someone cared about them. They had to hear it spoken aloud. "We care about you and we love you." We all need to hear it in our lives; the children of South Simcoe simply needed to hear it more often.

Sometimes the anger and frustration within the children would suddenly ignite a dangerous situation without warning. When this occurred, our teachers needed to draw upon their own good judgement and basic common sense to defuse the situation. Nothing in the background of Kim Kelly, who taught Grade Seven, could have prepared her for the day a student exploded in anger, withdrew a rusty razor blade from his pocket, stared her in the eyes and said, "I have a razor . . . and I can get you."

What was Kim to do? Run from the room? Call me for advice? There was no time. Instead, Kim stood her ground while the boy waved the razor at her, and she said, "You are making a bad choice, Carl. And you are making your problem bigger than it was before."

It took some time for her quiet message to sink in. Eventually, Carl put the razor away, Kim alerted the office, then she quietly resumed the class lesson. Later, when we discussed Carl's actions in detail, I assured her that we had taken prescribed action with authorities to prevent such an event from occurring again.

Years later, when we were reminiscing together about our time at South Simcoe, Kim always focused on the good things that happened in the school, rarely mentioning incidents such as the confrontation with Carl. "The thing I remember most," she said, "was the team atmosphere, and how we all were dedicated, in our own individual way, to helping those kids. We shared resources, we exchanged ideas, we laughed together, we cried together, we ate together—there was always food and celebration. And we made a difference, didn't we?"

I was constantly impressed by the staff's creative thinking and their practical solutions to problems. Sally Roberts, for example, was an enormously gifted and dedicated teacher with a knack for encouraging her Grade Three students to discover the joys of writing. When one boy appeared to have a deep-seated fear of putting anything on paper, Sally developed a game in which each of them took turns speaking a word aloud before making a sentence. The boy would start with a single word, perhaps "The," and Sally would ask him to write it down. Then she would say a second word, maybe "cat," and ask him to write it down as well. Next it was his turn to choose a word, speak it aloud and add it to the others. Eventually, of course, he would have a complete sentence written on paper, and they would work this way to create another sentence, and then another, until they had constructed an entire story.

The boy blossomed under Sally's warmth and guidance. By the end of the year he was able to write a complete eight-paragraph essay on a tropical rain forest, a topic that had fascinated him during his social studies class.

Individual attention proved endlessly rewarding and productive. Tom was a difficult student in Kim Kelly's Grade Seven class. Along with his disruptive behaviour, he demonstrated serious reading problems. Were the two situations connected? I have no doubt they were. Tom's struggles to read at the same level as his classmates made him feel insecure and a failure, and soon he refused even to attempt reading. Nothing seemed to work until one day Kim overheard Tom speaking with great enthusiasm about fishing. The next day Kim arrived in class with some fishing magazines, helped Tom get started on reading one of the articles, then stood back to watch him absorb everything he could about fishing. Tom was motivated to read because one teacher took the time, and made the effort, to spot a breakthrough point.

Jacki had a knack for winning kids to her side. She would use pet names when addressing them—David would become "Davey," for example. It may seem like a small, silly thing among all the other teaching methods available, but the children appreciated her nicknames for what they were: terms of endearment, a kind of shorthand that said, "I like you. You matter to me. You are a good kid."

Few of us tire of being told we are loved, that we matter, that someone cares about us. To children who might rarely, if ever, receive these messages at home, Jacki's simple use of pet names was a tonic, and another reason to value and enjoy every hour spent at South Simcoe.

We were more than a teaching staff. We were a team, and the difference between the two is much more than just semantics.

All of us were committed to making a difference to the kids in South Simcoe. But we also accepted responsibility for each other in a way that only the most fortunate and successful teams experience. This made it easier to maintain a warm smile for everyone—for each other, for parents and visitors, and most importantly, for the children. We began to be called "The school where everyone is always smiling," and the description included both the kids and the staff members. Our constant smiles were never forced. Thanks to the way we felt about ourselves, and the way the children and community responded, they just came naturally to us.

The family atmosphere at the school deepened and widened with time. At the end of one school day a student burst into my office to announce that the Prime Minister had arrived and was sitting in his limousine right outside the front door. The Prime Minister of Canada? Had our fame spread so far, and so fast?

I followed the boy down the hall to the door, and sure enough, a white stretch limousine was parked at the curb, the motor idling and a uniformed driver behind the wheel. The children could barely contain their excitement, climbing on the hood and trunk, stroking and sniffing the finish—one child even licked it! They had never seen such an impressive vehicle. If the Prime Minister was not inside, it had to be some celebrity, maybe even an entire rock band—the car was that big!

I knocked on the window to see who was inside. When the window rolled down, I was surprised to see not the Prime Minister but the boyfriend of one of our teachers, grinning at me from the back seat. He had a special surprise for her, and I had a good idea what it might be. When the teacher finally emerged and climbed into the limo, the children all cheered as they drove away to a special dinner, where her boyfriend proposed to her.

We all joined in the preparations for the marriage, planning teas and choosing gifts as though it were our own sister and not just a member of our staff who was being wed. Later, when the teacher was hospitalized for over three months while pregnant with her first child, at least one staff member visited her, or called at least once, every day of the week. We took the same personal interest in all the children born to staff members. They became South Simcoe Babies, and we shared in the joy of their arrival.

As time passed, we discovered the impact our approach was making on the students—sometimes with touching results.

One day, in the middle of an otherwise uneventful afternoon, my door opened and Sally entered. Her face was white, her hands were trembling, and she looked as though she were about to burst into tears. "I've done something terrible," she said. Sally was a wonderful, caring teacher, one of the strongest supporters of our program at South Simcoe.

I urged her to sit down, handed her some tissues and asked her to explain what had happened.

"I told a student to shut up," she confessed. "I said 'Please shut up!' but still it was 'Shut up!' and I feel so badly about it."

Telling anyone to shut up meant breaking an important agreement at South Simcoe. Children had agreed not to say the "S" phrase to teachers, and teachers had agreed not to say it to children. It violated our basic principle of maintaining equal respect on all sides. Sally knew this, and nothing I said would make her feel any better—or any worse.

Once the words were out of her mouth, Sally did the same thing we advised students to do after an angry outburst: she went to a quiet place, leaving the room until she regained her composure. I reminded Sally that she was a wonderful teacher; she had simply lost her cool and made a mistake. "We all make mistakes," I assured her. "Stay here until you feel ready, then go back to the classroom and explain it to the students."

And Sally did. She explained that she had made a mistake and asked the class to help her decide how to make amends,

When she finished, a seven year old in her class proved the children understood our guiding principles when she approached Sally and said: "It's all right, Miss Roberts. You made a mistake. We'll just have to help you manage your frustration better so it doesn't happen again."

Sally, as she explained to me later, didn't know whether to laugh or cry.

I cannot overemphasize the importance of the warm environment we managed to create among the staff and, to a remarkable degree, among the children as well. We admitted as much sunlight into the rooms as possible, using plants and flowers to add warmth. We created a Bouquet Board, where staff members could post written congratulations and thankyous to each other recognizing achievements with students, events in their lives, and little favours performed.

Like all families, we encountered crises. And like all warm and caring families, we helped each other through them.

When Michelle arrived at South Simcoe to teach, she quickly fit into the group. The children loved her bubbly and bright personality every bit as much as the rest of the staff. Within a few months, however, Michelle began to have difficulties. First, she started forgetting things. Most of us would laugh off these incidents, saying we were all simply becoming too busy, or that it was due to stress and overload. But Michelle's father had been diagnosed with Alzheimer's, and she spent evenings and weekends caring for him, which not only heightened her awareness of the disease but also placed intense pressure on her ability to handle her teaching workload. Then, just when it seemed she couldn't possibly handle another source of stress, her marriage began to collapse.

All of this began to affect her work. How could it not? Eventually I had to discuss the situation with her. Her only solution, she felt, was to leave the school, but I refused to accept that. Michelle often told me her work was emotionally draining, which was not surprising news. On very bad days, I told myself the same thing. "But the emotionally draining part can become the uplifting part as well," I argued. "We have highs and we have lows here. The lows are tough, but the highs are wonderful. Besides, you know how hard we all work to keep each other's spirits up. You can count on receiving love and support here as much as the children do."

Then I added: "Remember what Sharon always says?"

She smiled and nodded. Sharon McLean often said, "We crash, but we don't burn." She meant that we often encountered challenges that put us off the track or left us feeling dismayed and even helpless for a while. But we always recovered, because we always looked out for each other. When someone needed an emotional boost, they could count on receiving it from another staff member, or sometimes the entire staff. We took responsibility for one another's welfare; it was the glue that held us together.

I shook my head. "I can't let you go," I said.

She promised to stay if I would help her, and of course I did.

We all lent Michelle our support. I would stop by her classroom twice each day to remind her how much she was valued and how many people cared about her. When passing her in the hall, I would give her a thumbs-up signal to lift her spirits.

Experiences like Michelle's strengthened the team and improved our dedication to the children. "Don't give up on them," I kept reminding everyone. "Don't give up on any of them." When we refused to give up on Michelle, and she responded by becoming an even better teacher, we proved our point all over again: Adults need support every bit as much as children do.

I began ending our staff meetings on an uplifting note by reading an appropriate passage from an appropriate book or essay. After dealing with challenges for a solid hour, many of them emotionally draining at times, it was important to have everyone leave the room in a positive frame of mind.

This led to our Wonderful Wednesday sessions, when we would gather on that day to absorb good thoughts and generate inner strength among us. Usually I would read from an inspiring book, and we would all discuss the significance of the words and ideas to us, and how we could apply them to improve our lives and the lives of the children entrusted to our care. The topics were always relevant to us as individuals and teachers, such as handling stress, strengthening the spirit and living each day with happiness.

Now and then, I encountered teachers from other schools with special points of view on these topics, and invited them to visit us and deliver their thoughts in person.

We didn't stop there. We began assembling a library of books on uplifting topics. We displayed quotations and proverbs in the staff room, sayings that boosted our positive outlook and kept us focused on making a small difference in the lives of the children each day. We even created small rituals to strengthen the team, such as our end-of-term breakfast when, on the last day of every school term, we arrived at 7 A.M., all decked out in the school colours, for a celebration breakfast.

The word "team" sounds almost inadequate to describe the strength and support we offered, and drew from, one another as a result of these activities. It was a deeply emotional experience and one, I believe, that was responsible for much of our success at South Simcoe.

The staff were unique individuals. As teachers, they brought a varied background and depth of experience to their work. But their responses to many of my proposals were just as varied, and my experiences with Jacki, Randy and Frank are three very different examples.

Jacki Devolin was a classroom assistant, and at first this made her reluctant to participate in many of the programs we launched. Since she did not carry a teacher's qualifications, she often backed away from speaking her mind or assuming certain duties. But I encouraged her, pointing out that everyone was an important part of the team. As long as we all kept our focus on what was best for the children, we each had a right to comment and make suggestions.

It took time to help Jacki overcome her inhibitions, follow her heart and not just stick to her job description. When she did participate fully, the transformation was astonishing. Almost overnight Jacki became everyone's mom. We all, staff and students, felt comfortable confiding in her—including me, by the way—knowing she would listen and offer her wise advice. She also began to demonstrate a wonderful knack for organization, and no event at South Simcoe was launched without Jacki's meticulous approach to planning and scheduling.

In sharp contrast to Jacki, Randy Weekes needed a mere invitation to become an active member of the team. Randy was the chief custodian at South Simcoe and quickly warmed to the idea of attending staff meetings, enthusiastically adding his ideas and suggestions. He and Gail, of course, had been the original inspiration behind our successful Gold Dustpan Award. A dedicated environmentalist, Randy began building birdhouses, bat-houses and other projects with the children, using recycled wood, and he started a garden with plants specially chosen to attract butterflies. Eventually he formed an Environmental Club with the students, teaching them about environmental issues and setting up a program for them to recycle paper, plastic, glass and other items.

Randy made an impact across the city. When he saw the positive results of our gardening efforts at South Simcoe, he contacted all the other school custodians along Simcoe Street and suggested they plant gardens in front of their schools, using flowers that repeated their school colours. A few years later Mayor Nancy Diamond reminded me that, thanks to our school custodian, the entire city of Oshawa had grown more beautiful.

Jacki had been a classroom assistant, afraid at first to act like a teacher. Randy was a custodian who could hardly wait to add his contribution to the children's education.

And then there was Frank.

From the first time he heard me discuss my plans for South Simcoe, Frank made no effort to hide his skepticism. When I tried to explain my reasoning, he would remind me of the extra years of experience he had, as well as his deeper understanding of the community. "You just don't understand these people," he would say. "Not like I do. You have to be firm with the kids. Start suspending more of them. And start supporting me, because I know things about this neighbourhood that you don't know."

I suppose I realized from the start that Frank was never going to see things my way. I was unable to hide my resentment and Frank could not conceal his animosity. The result was that neither of us handled the dispute as well as we might have, and Frank chose to transfer to another school at the end of that first year.

He wasn't the only one to leave, in disagreement with me. Three members of the teaching staff chose to leave at the end of my first year, so I spent a good deal of time interviewing and hiring candidates to replace them. I wanted bright, energetic and enthusiastic people, of course, but more than that, I wanted people who cared as passionately about the children and their welfare as Sharon McLean did. They needed teamwork skills as well. I expected them to feel comfortable functioning not only with me and the other staff members, but also with parents and members of the community generally. Finally, I looked for candidates who were enthusiastic about teaching—whose greatest joy was experiencing the thrill of discovery on a child's face when he or she masters a new skill, like reading a difficult passage or understanding some mathematical process. They would see teaching as a calling of the heart as well as a profession, and their talents would spring from the heart and soul as much as the mind.

I finally selected three new teachers, and I am proud to say that they all became caught up in the special climate we were seeking to establish at South Simcoe Public School.

Still, others would leave over the years, and the losses hurt me. Colleagues and friends warned that this would happen; you cannot, after all, expect everyone to grasp a new idea with equal levels of enthusiasm. And I make no apologies for being demanding and strong-willed. Still, I regret losing the experience that Frank and others might have brought to our venture.

Chapter 5

We Love, We Listen, We Share

*W*ith the school building more attractive and efficient, and the teaching staff encouraged by our early successes, I turned my attention to another critical element: participation by the parents. Their support was essential. We needed the parents not only to understand our teaching strategies but to offer their support and encouragement as well.

Once again, as principal, I received a harsh lesson in reality.

At every other school in my experience there had always been a core group of parents who responded enthusiastically whenever called upon by teachers or principal to attend a school meeting and discuss their children's progress. School meetings were both a social event and an opportunity to assess the children's progress and the school's operation.

At South Simcoe many parents not only failed to attend such meetings, but they refused to even answer telephone calls from the school. This seemed strange until I discovered that several homes subscribed to call display, which was carefully scrutinized before the receiver was lifted. My immediate reaction, of course, was irritation at their spendthrift ways. How could these people afford a luxury like call display when they seemed to lack the resources to feed and clothe their own children?

Eventually I learned why. Many of the parents who would not answer the telephone were single mothers, and they used call display to avoid speaking to threatening or abusive former husbands or ex-boyfriends. Call display was no luxury, but a defence. If her child was exhibiting behavioural problems, a mother didn't want to be asked to come to the school and retrieve her child. She had enough of her own problems to deal with, and preferred that the school deal with the child, at least for a few hours each day. When she saw that South Simcoe Public School was calling, she simply assumed it was bad news about her kid, which she could do without.

Even parents who chose to answer my telephone calls failed to respond in the expected manner. During our telephone conversation, some became non-communicative, reluctant to discuss any aspect of their child's schooling. Others were defensive and even abusive, actually shouting and cursing before hanging up.

I refused to be discouraged. I had seen how beautiful and promising many of our students were. Without the participation of parents, the children would never realize all their potential during their time at South Simcoe. I determined not to give up; I needed the parents to work with me and help me.

We implemented a strategy I had introduced at other schools, making "Sunshine Calls" to parents who actually answered the telephone. A Sunshine Call conveyed good news about the progress of their children, and I encouraged every teacher to make several each week. Remembering my mother's lecture about the unexpected Christmas doll, I suggested that the staff find something good to say about each child. It needn't be restricted to learning progress, I advised. Children could be praised for asking questions, for being pleasant to other students, or for always smiling. This good news could serve as a conversation-opener, leading to other discussions and building a relationship with the parent.

The first few Sunshine Calls incurred suspicion, and even disbelief that teachers would phone parents to share good news about the results of a test or the completion of a reading assignment. Eventually the calls became welcomed, especially when parents heard teachers say, "I just want you to know that I'm delighted to be teaching your child this year," or a similar statement.

By the end of the first month of school, we agreed that each teacher would contact the parent of every child in his or her class. We also insisted that every parent attend the school at the end of the first term for the December report-card interview, where the students could show off the work in their portfolios and share their success.

As I suspected, word of our Sunshine Calls spread among parents in the neighbourhood. One parent would tell another that their child's teacher had called home, not to complain about Sammy or Emma, but to say how much they enjoyed teaching him or her. How about that? they might comment. Isn't that different? Even some parents with call display began to risk answering a telephone call from South Simcoe to learn that, yes, their child was doing well.

When contact between parents and school was no longer seen as a method of conveying bad news, conversations between teacher and parent became more pleasant, almost social in nature. Sunshine Calls represented a major step towards creating a level of parent and community involvement that still astounds many people, and frankly, continues to surprise me a little as well.

By this time I had grown very proud of the South Simcoe staff. Teaching, especially at a school like South Simcoe, can be an intense and emotionally draining process, one that usually extends the teachers' work hours well into the evenings and weekends. Making their first Sunshine Calls, often from their own home during the evening, was not an easy thing for many of the staff members to do. I'm sure they would have preferred to spend the time with their spouse and family, or reading a book, or just relaxing. But because they knew it made a difference to the children, the staff took the time to make these calls, displaying a wonderful level of commitment and dedication. Their actions opened the door to so much that we accomplished at South Simcoe, and I remain very proud of the teachers to this day.

I wanted the special give-and-take atmosphere of a dynamic meeting between parents and educators. I sent every South Simcoe child home with an invitation for their parents to gather at the school for a meeting in a few days' time, where we would enjoy coffee, snacks and conversation. I anticipated a turnout of perhaps twenty parents, which would make a good-sized group for discussion. On the day of the meeting I arrived early to make gallons of coffee and set out plates of food. At my previous school these sessions were always well attended, with some parents inviting friends along as company.

The time for our get-together came . . . and passed. No one arrived. They may just be late, I thought, and I stood at the window looking this way and that, up and down the street—but not a parent appeared.

I asked Joan if she had any messages for me from parents. Didn't anyone at least call and send their regrets?

Not one.

I sat and drank three cups of coffee alone. What had gone wrong? Were the parents so unconcerned about their children that they couldn't be bothered to attend a meeting? Later, I discovered that parents in the South Simcoe neighbourhood looked upon an invitation from the principal as a sign of trouble. It's no wonder they chose not to respond. Who wants to spend time in a school hearing bad news about their kids?

Over the next few days I spoke to parents as they arrived at school to escort their children home, hoping to explain that meeting in my office did not mean their child was in trouble at all. I approached one mother and invited her to meet me for coffee and a chat. Her response was frankly rude.

"Why should I talk to you?" she said. "I've got better things to do."

The next woman was just as brusque. "Leave me alone," she said. "I don't want to see you. I'm not in trouble."

Another woman told me that she didn't want to talk to me because she didn't have a problem. "But when I do," she warned, "you'll be hearing from me!"

Some parents, thank goodness, heard me out, and out of perhaps two dozen that I approached, three agreed to come inside for coffee and a chat. But even they were suspicious of my motives. "Why are we really here?" one parent asked.

I began by describing our goals for the school. I told them why we had put so much effort into sprucing up the school, and explained our logo and motto, *Together We Light the Way*. I mentioned how we stressed respect in the school, why we needed to focus on academic skills as well as respect, teamwork and leadership, and discussed how we were setting goals for everyone to achieve. Achieving goals creates a sense of accomplishment and pride, and pride in oneself is a key to many things—happiness, self-respect, respect for others, and so on. Then I asked how the parents felt about the idea.

There was a long silence before one woman said, in genuine surprise, "You mean you want our opinion?"

I told her I certainly did.

She began with a list of all the things she did not like. She did not like the way children were free to walk around the room, and she did not like the idea of children working in groups instead of sitting in rows and concentrating on their work, which was the way she had been taught.

I patiently explained that we used a variety of teaching strategies and techniques, because children learn in so many different ways. Children were not wandering about the room willy-nilly; they were working in groups to exchange ideas and solve problems. Working in groups taught them the concept of teamwork and permitted each child to enhance his or her learning style through co-operative learning. There were different ways to teach different children, I pointed out, and co-operative learning was a very powerful method for children to learn respect for others in the classroom.

I kept the explanations simple, and when the parents seemed keenly interested in my words, I proposed that we meet on a regular basis.

"How often?" one parent asked.

I asked how often the group felt would be both necessary and convenient. We agreed on once a month.

Half an hour had passed and no one seemed in a hurry to leave, so I suggested they remain and discuss their children's education for as long as they liked. They stayed two hours, sipping coffee, discussing the challenges of raising and educating children, and gradually warming to the idea of becoming more involved in helping to make decisions regarding the school's activities.

Finally, one of the parents suggested we might want a name for the meetings, and someone said, "How about Parent Rap?" Parent Rap it was. We agreed that it would be a forum for exchanging ideas, an opportunity for everyone to become involved in decision-making and a chance to work out problems involving all the children in the school.

Although I had recruited only three parents to this point, I was elated at the kind of discussion we launched during that first session and I made the Parent Rap meetings a top priority.

At one early session a mother who was joining the group for the first time arrived upset with me, and quickly began explaining why.

"I ordered my daughter to finish eating her food," she said, bristling. "When she didn't, I got angry with her and told her she damn well better finish it. And do you know what she said? She told me that I had no right to swear at her like that. She said it wasn't respectful. I asked who told her that, and she said, 'Mrs. Dean says I have the right to be respected, and nobody has the right to yell or swear at me.'" The mother narrowed her eyes. "Is that the kind of stuff you're teaching here?" she demanded.

"As a matter of fact," I said calmly, "it is."

To my great relief and satisfaction the other parents began defending me, explaining how respect for everyone was the basis for all we were trying to accomplish at the school. If you respect children, they will begin to respect you, they told her.

It felt good to hear them say those words. Their reaction was one more measure of the way we were starting to change things at South Simcoe.

Despite their comments, by the end of my first year at South Simcoe I began wondering if Parent Rap was worth the effort we were putting into it. Sunshine Calls and invitations were helping build relationships with parents, but they were not successful in actually bringing large numbers of moms and dads into the school. All of our programs, I knew, would be enhanced so much if we could just generate wider involvement from the parents.

"Do you really think we should continue with these meetings?" I asked at the last Parent Rap session in June. "There have only been three of you here for the sessions."

"Don't give up yet," one parent responded. "We love the time we spend here and the way we can talk so openly." Another suggested that we set a goal of doubling the attendance at Parent Rap by Christmas.

The parents began actively to spread the word throughout the neighbourhood. Parent Rap was fun, they told everyone. You get to enjoy coffee and snacks, and the principal is there to talk with you. You learn a lot about your kids' education too. Wasn't that worth an hour a month?

By Christmas we had exceeded our goal, and the group continued to grow rapidly with every session. Encouraged, I began recruiting contributions of perfume, cosmetic soap bars and coffee mugs from various sources, distributing them at our meetings. I also invited speakers from a number of organizations to discuss medical emergencies, strategies for dealing with daily stress, babysitting concerns and other topics. All of this built an even larger Parent Rap group, creating a momentum that encouraged parents to continue to offer their own suggestions about school policy and programs.

We made it as easy and convenient as possible for parents to attend. Some parents, for example, were able to attend only when they brought their preschool children to the Parent Rap sessions. This prompted us to invite St. John's Ambulance members to train students to babysit the children, providing the parents with time to concentrate on topics concerning their older children at South Simcoe.

Eventually, Parent Rap became not just a school-focused event but a community-based organization dedicated to improving the quality of life throughout the South Simcoe neighbourhood. Our sessions proved to be powerful motivators for parents to accept greater responsibility, not only for their children but also for their own welfare, in order to fulfill their responsibilities as parents.

We always tried to respond to their needs. When the parents asked for help in streetproofing their children, we invited a police officer to discuss the topic with them. When the parents said they didn't understand what the report cards were saying, we dropped the jargon and made the language simple and easy to understand.

A range of speakers arrived at Parent Rap, and their topics would have done Oprah proud. The mother of one of our teachers, a retired bank manager, arrived to explain how to prepare and manage a home budget. A nutritionist discussed planning and preparing healthy, low-cost family meals, and explained the connection between good nutrition and learning ability. Other speakers demonstrated how to read food packaging to obtain top value for every dollar spent.

Pam Anderson, a banker, spoke to parents about employ-ability skills and the importance of understanding new job technology. When she invited the parents to visit her in a gleaming downtown Toronto bank tower to experience the technology first-hand, many accepted with enthusiasm.

We didn't always go outside the group for speakers. Some of the Parent Rap members had skills and knowledge of their own to share, and they did, with enthusiasm and per-sonal satisfaction. When the government slashed social assis-tance payments, it was the members of Parent Rap who prepared a community directory of social services in the area. This directory was also used in a number of other Oshawa-area schools—a nice tribute to their talents.

I wanted the discussions at Parent Rap to be open and lively, with a healthy airing of different opinions and differ-ent points of view. And they were—which naturally led to a few tense moments in the early sessions.

To keep the "Say what you think" atmosphere but avoid confrontations, we developed a series of ground rules for successful interaction:

- *We are partners.* We will work together to discuss issues, reach decisions and solve problems—all to improve the education and well-being of our children.

- *We respect.* We recognize that everyone has the right to be respected, and we accept the responsibility to treat each other in a respectful manner.

- *We love and we care.* We will work in a loving, caring and supportive manner to provide a loving, caring environment for our children.

- *We value everyone.* We realize that everyone has a role
  to play. Therefore, we will accept, appreciate and
  value everyone's opinions and ideas.

To demonstrate that I appreciated just how stressful parenting can be, we held special sessions to address questions of personal well-being, dealing with stress and taking time to nurture yourself.

Parent Rap grew into a very powerful way of building relationships between parents, the school and the wider community, and many Parent Rap members became strong advocates for the school.

I began to wonder who was learning more from this experience—me or the parents? In spite of my beliefs about equality, I had to admit I arrived at South Simcoe with some preconceived ideas about the parents of the students. Among them was the possibility that the residents weren't taking enough responsibility for their children and placed too little value on education. The underlying message was: *Why can't they just improve their lives? Then they could help their own kids.*

This attitude is not, I'm sorry to say, rare among middle-class people who have never found themselves in situations of economic stress, or who have never been deprived of emotional support. It is very common for them to look at many residents of the South Simcoe neighbourhood and similar areas and ask, "Why can't they pick themselves up by their bootstraps?" or "How can they choose to live the way they do?"

I often felt the same way. Until I met people like Sylvia.

Sylvia's son Mark, a Grade Four student, suffered from severe learning problems. Mark could neither read nor write and, what's more, he didn't seem to care. Both Mark's teacher and I proposed placing the boy in a special class where he could receive special help, but try as we might, Sylvia refused to permit it.

I persuaded Sylvia to visit me in my office, where I planned to carefully explain the opportunity for individual teaching in a smaller classroom and suggest that it was the best solution we could offer for Mark's difficulties. But no matter how I spelled out the benefits for Mark, I could not persuade Sylvia to see our point of view. Sylvia grew more and more adamant about refusing to admit Mark to a special class and, I must admit, I became more and more impatient with her. I simply could not understand why she did not want her son to benefit from this approach.

Finally, Sylvia opened up with a tragic story that explained her reluctance and forced me to reassess my perception of her and other parents. Sylvia told me that her sister, while still a very young child, had been diagnosed as mentally handicapped. "She threw a lot of temper tantrums," Sylvia said, "and she was hard for my parents to control. So they locked her up. She was just a little child, and they took her away to a home with other people who they thought were crazy too."

Recalling her sister's story after all these years was painful, but Sylvia kept going. "When she was an adult," Sylvia said, trying to maintain her composure, "after she had spent all her childhood years in this home for the mentally handicapped, some doctors took another look at her case." Tears began streaming down Sylvia's face. "And do you know what they found out? They found out that my sister had never been mentally handicapped. She was close to normal intelligence. She just had some hearing problems. She never should have been put away like that. But by then it was too late."

I listened to her tale with growing horror. As a result of all the years confined in the company of truly handicapped people, Sylvia's sister had acquired strange mannerisms that made others uncomfortable in her presence. Sylvia had not been mentally handicapped when admitted, and she was not mentally handicapped as an adult. But she appeared as though she were, and the appearance was so disturbing that she could not be considered a candidate for early release.

"First it cost my sister her childhood," Sylvia said through her tears, "and then it cost her her freedom. And why? Because somebody looked at her as a little child and decided she should be put away from the other kids. Now do you see why I don't want my son placed in a segregated class?"

Of course I did. I didn't agree with her decision, but I now understood her opposition to the idea. Sylvia wasn't refusing to agree to his transfer out of stubbornness or ignorance. She was doing it out of love. She wanted to protect Mark from risking the same horrible treatment Sylvia's sister had received, because she could no longer trust the system to do the correct thing.

Sylvia's story brought tears to my eyes as well, and we cried together there in my office, without shame. I placed my arm around her shoulders. "Do you know what I see here?" I said. "I see a mother who loves her child very much. I thought you didn't care about your son. I'm sorry I misjudged you."

My words generated some trust in her, because Sylvia agreed that we could at least identify Mark as a student in need of special assistance. We struck a compromise, and Mark eventually began to receive remedial attention.

I think of Sylvia and her sister whenever I hear people discuss the problems of disadvantaged people as though the solution were merely a matter of courage, determination or money. They cannot grasp the idea that disadvantaged people need support—emotional, economic, educational, or in other forms—to reach their full potential.

More and more I began to appreciate the complexity of the issues facing families. As a society, we applaud alcoholics who seek support from AA, drug addicts who go looking for assistance from physicians, and smokers who rely on their families or stop-smoking groups to break the nicotine habit. But when support for broken, disadvantaged families is proposed, some voices invariably protest against the idea.

That's very sad, don't you think?

• • • • • •

Chapter 6

"Not *My* Kids. *Our* Kids!"

*M*y childhood in Trinidad was influenced, one way or another, by everyone in our community. The African proverb "It takes a village to raise a child" has become something of a cliché, but like all clichés it happens to be true. In Trinidad we could always count on neighbours for support when we needed it, just as our neighbours knew they could count on us. Children everywhere need this kind of support from their communities. Life has become too complex for any single group to care for children and address their needs.

Yet I sensed a reluctance among people to reach out to their neighbours in the South Simcoe neighbourhood. Some of this, of course, was due to the transient nature of the people who lived there. It takes time to build relationships among adults (children seem to do it so quickly and naturally!), and some families simply didn't remain in one place long enough to get to know their neighbours, much less count on them.

I was determined, naturally, that South Simcoe Public School would become the centre of its community, a place where everyone could put their heads together and make decisions that were in the best interests of the children. I drew on my personal feelings about asking for help, starting with our lack of a proper meeting room. During the first several months the only place we could meet within the school was in the hallway; it was the only space large enough to accommodate the entire group of students and teachers, and it simply would not do. In order to create a team spirit, we needed a place to meet as an entire school for assemblies and concerts and, most of all, to celebrate our successes.

The nearby Legion Hall had been used by the school a few times in the past for graduation exercises. Why not ask if we could use it on a regular basis? I wondered. The manager's own child had attended South Simcoe Public School years before, when the area had been a thriving community, a place where children had felt safe, protected and loved. So he had a special appreciation for our efforts to restore that environment for the students.

He agreed to let us use the hall, reserving the right to review the situation each month, and asking that we leave the room as clean as we found it. Of course we would—and did. This was the first step in our partnership efforts, which forged an amazing bond between the school and the surrounding community.

Once we had a place where we could meet as a team, gather to listen to speakers, and generally to feel united as a school, we grew even closer. Meanwhile, the manager began spreading news of the school's achievements among the Legion members. With time, the members saw South Simcoe children not as kids who might wreck their hall, but as basically decent children who simply needed support and attention. Once that idea was firmly planted, the Legion members began reaching out to us. What did we think of some war veterans visiting the school on Remembrance Day to talk to our students and tell them personal stories of World War II, the Korean War and other conflicts? Naturally, we thought it would be wonderful: there could be no better way for children to appreciate the sacrifices these men and others of their generation had made, and to bring history alive.

Their visits were followed by other offers from the Legion members, who donated stacks of *National Geographic* magazines and supported a wide range of school events throughout the year. Soon, four Kiwanis Club members who had formed a band called The Three Harmony Cats and One Dog Drummer began performing for our children, who sang along and accompanied the musicians with percussion instruments. The music from our intergenerational band may not have been concert-hall quality, unless you measure harmony and rhythm according to the level of joy it creates, but these performances were great fun for everyone involved, and the mutual joy created between people separated by several decades is something to behold.

As we began to acknowledge all the assistance available to us from the surrounding community, we agreed on some guidelines about the kind of help and support we wanted. We did not, for example, want either the school or the children to be considered "charity cases." We sought people and organizations who would abide by our guiding principles, who believed in the same things as we did, and who were prepared to go the extra mile or so to reach a goal. We wanted support from those who believed in our kids, and who would help us bring out all the energy and potential within our students so that they could grow and develop and take their place in the community. In summary, we wanted long-term partnerships with these people.

Too many of the kids had already suffered abandonment of one kind or another in their short lives, and we didn't want to risk the effect of having new people move into their lives briefly before vanishing forever. We wanted help from people who agreed to be there for the long haul.

The Legion Hall was just to the north of the school. In the opposite direction, and directly across the street, sat a strip mall, and I remembered how my heart sank at the first sight of it. Malls represent tempting opportunities for students, ranging from loitering to outright vandalism and theft. Even though we continued to make steady progress with our kids, the mall presented as big a problem to us as many of the kids did to the merchants.

Shoplifting by South Simcoe students and other kids in the community was a major headache for the store owners. Things grew complicated when the owners were both unable to contact the parents and reluctant to call the police. Invariably, they turned to us. Or more precisely, to me.

"We caught another one of your kids shoplifting over here," a store manager might say to me over the telephone. "Why can't the school do something about them?"

The first few times I heard this, I naturally felt distressed, and perhaps a little guilty because I hadn't solved the problem. As time went on, I grew more and more frustrated, until one day when yet another merchant called to complain about "your kids." Slipping into my coat, I marched across the street to the mall and entered his store. I try to control my temper at all times, but I must admit I was close to losing it on this occasion.

"Look," I said to the store manager, "I'm tired of being called to come and pick up *my* kids. These are not just *my* kids. They are *our* kids. They live around here. Their parents shop here. They are every bit as much a part of this community as you are. So instead of expecting me to solve the problem on my own, why don't you offer to help me?"

"OK," the manager said calmly. "What do you want me to do?"

His cool and helpful response was unexpected, and I was taken aback for a moment. The man was offering to help me solve a major problem. "Let me think about it," I said, "and I'll get back to you."

Returning to my office, I gave the idea some thought. If the Legion could become partners and actively involved in our activities, why not the store owners?

The first thing to do, I decided, was not to take the children over to the mall—that was hardly necessary, after all—but to invite the merchants into the school, where we could put our heads together and come up with some sort of plan.

I approached the manager of the Swiss Chalet restaurant in the mall, a man named Phil Lawson. He would be, I feared, a hard sell. The kids often amused themselves by loosening lids on his salt and pepper shakers, and similar stunts that created constant headaches for him and his staff. But Phil surprised me by quickly agreeing that we had to put our collective heads together and find a way to deal with our problem.

At our first meeting Phil suggested that if he and other mall merchants would cross the street, enter the school and speak to the children in their own environment, perhaps the children would be more respectful. They would begin to see the merchants as friends and neighbours. Phil's biggest concern was that the children might ask him some tough questions.

"If they do," I assured him, "I'll be there to help you answer them, assuming they're not too tough for me as well."

He was a hit! During his talk to our Grade Eight students, Phil talked about employability and the value of entrepreneurial skills. He even suggested some of the students might run a restaurant like his one day. "And if you do," he said, "I know you'll want everyone to treat you with respect." When he finished, the children swamped him with all sorts of questions, some amusing, some provocative and some rather profound. Phil treated them all seriously, listening carefully and answering in as much detail as the children could understand.

When the presentation concluded and the children returned to their class, buzzing with excitement about all they had learned, I posed a question of my own. What would he think, I asked Phil, about pairs of Grade Eight students actually visiting behind the scenes at his restaurant for short periods of time during the school day, to observe the kinds of activities he had just described?

"Why not?" he said. "We can at least try it."

It became much more than an experiment; it grew into one of the most rewarding programs we launched at South Simcoe. Suddenly the children realized that teamwork and respect were not just ideas cooked up by the teachers to keep everyone organized and respectful in the classroom. They were considered important talents and values by society generally. Even something as simple as assembling and serving a salad meant accepting responsibility and trusting others to do their job correctly, especially when the salad was to be served to several dozen people. They also recognized the intangible rewards that meaningful work can bring. I asked Samuel, one of the first group of students to visit the restaurant, what he enjoyed most. "It was fun making the food, and then watching people eat it," he said. "They liked the food, and I wanted to go up and say, 'I'm glad you like it... because I made it!'"

Before each visit to Phil's restaurant the students were prepared by their teachers to observe how the lessons taught in the classroom about Respect, Teamwork and Leadership were applied outside the school. Phil took the time to explain the work, why it was important, and how everyone on the restaurant staff counted on each other—which reinforced everything we had been teaching.

Very quickly we saw positive changes take place on both sides of the fence. The small acts of vandalism at Swiss Chalet virtually disappeared, because the manager and staff were now friends with the students. Phil developed a special kinship with the children. It was no longer *your* kids, but *our* kids. "How are our kids doing?" he might say when we met. He also saw them as individuals, with special personalities and skills. "How's that little Sammy doing?" he would ask. "Boy, he asks a lot of questions! And how about Charmaine? She says she wants to be a waitress, but I told her she's bright enough to run this place." Whenever Phil entered the school, children ran up to shake his hands and say, "Hi, Mr. Lawson! How's business?"

Later, Phil arranged for the Swiss Chalet chicken mascot to participate in several events at the school. Whether it was the unusual sight of an adult-sized costumed chicken or the goodwill generated from Phil's support for the school, the Swiss Chalet chicken brought more than excitement and popularity with him. Whenever the chicken planted a flower in our garden, for instance, it was remembered by the children as "one of the Chicken's flowers," and received extra care and attention.

From this rather uncertain beginning, we developed our Experiential Learning program, now called Connections: Classroom and Community, one of the most extraordinary initiatives undertaken at South Simcoe. Later, we extended the program to include not only Grade Seven students and businesses in the neighbouring mall, but major corporations. This later involvement focused on building partnerships and developing relationships with individuals in each organization, rather than with the corporation as an entity.

Participation by these concerned and caring individuals varied widely, according to their situations. Some visited the school, working with our students, on a regular weekly basis. Others arrived less frequently, every few months perhaps, while many chose to work with us in a continuous advisory capacity, helping us in our strategic planning and program operations.

Instead of imposing our own ideas on the partners' activities, we always began by discussing the larger goals of the school and asking how each partner could assist us in achieving them. The result was an amazing collection of skills, each adding its own unique facet of aid and assistance to our programs.

Rob Pitfield, for example, an executive vice-president with ScotiaBank, arrived to read stories to our younger children. Soon, his visits included relating tales of his successes and achievements with Grade Seven students. The bonding between Rob and both groups of students was remarkable. When Rob invited the Grade One children to visit him at his office, they enthusiastically agreed and, on the scheduled day, were so excited that they burst in on an important meeting he was chairing with shouts of "Hi Rob!" and began describing him to the startled onlookers as "Our Rob. He's our Rob!" Rob, to his credit, accepted the interruption with his usual good grace and humour.

Another bank executive, Linda Sinclair, grew so impressed with our programs that she also invited students to visit her in her Royal Bank of Canada office. Later, I spoke to a group of Royal Bank's Ontario managers about setting and achieving goals. Terry Morgan, manager at the nearby Toronto-Dominion Bank, helped our senior classes learn how to open a bank account, write cheques, balance a chequebook, and establish and maintain a budget. Canada Trust, through their Friends of the Environment program, assisted the school in planting and maintaining the lovely flower gardens that gave so many people so much pleasure.

Tom McNoun, who was with the marketing division of General Motors of Canada, invited our Grade Eight class to GM's headquarters, where he showed how the same mathematical skills they were learning in class were being applied every day by GM employees. And when one of the science classes at our school was having difficulty grasping the concept of fuel, propulsion and energy, Tom arrived in person to explain the principles. I'm told that the children talked about his lesson for weeks afterward and, I suspect, will never forget it.

Barry Kuntz, with General Motors, arranged for his staff to provide a large tent at the school during our Community Days, where members of GM's Ontario zone arrived to read stories aloud to large groups of children who, of course, enjoyed it immensely.

Still with GM, Ann Nurse, owner of a local Saturn auto dealership, volunteered to speak on the importance of teamwork and the role it played in helping her firm provide satisfactory customer service. Ann also became a regular guest at our Circle of Love reading events.

It's difficult to exaggerate the value of these partnerships to the students, and their impact on the children. These were busy senior executives, often with roots far beyond the South Simcoe community, who believed it was important to contribute their time in this manner. Logic told the students that, if these partners felt it was important to do these things, the students themselves must be important, and the boost it provided to their self-worth was immeasurable.

On a more practical note, the children began to associate the skills and knowledge they were accumulating at school with their practical application. They also began to envision themselves in a variety of career situations, understanding how abstract concepts such as teamwork, respect and leadership skills were prized in the workplace and in society generally. The employees at GM and in the banks were analyzing graphs each day, just as the students were learning to do. And in the workplace or out of it, the children realized they would constantly need to make decisions, relate to the needs of others, build and maintain relationships, and appreciate and accept differences between individuals. All of these concepts were absorbed through the Connections program with amazing impact and conviction.

I'm the first to admit that Connections did not spring fully conceived from my mind. Frankly, it grew out of a practical need to reach beyond the school itself in search of assistance in helping the children to learn. No one, including me, could foresee the degree of its success and the way it generated rich rewards for everyone concerned. Most important of all, Connections demonstrated the benefits to be gained when schools, businesses and the community at large all work together to help children learn.

I wish I could say that the Connections program was responsible for totally eliminating all the problems our neighbours were having with South Simcoe students, but things are rarely that simple. It did make a significant difference, improving the awareness of the children about their own responsibilities, and changing the attitudes of mall merchants from suspicion and near outright hostility to understanding and co-operation. But problems lingered.

One Monday morning I arrived at school to discover that two Grade Eight boys had been caught shoplifting some items from one of the mall stores on the weekend. I called one of them, a cocky but, darn it, likeable boy named Jacques, into my office.

"Jacques," I said with great disappointment, "how could you do such a thing? You know these people by now. They are our friends and our neighbours. They have come into the school here and talked to us. They work with us here. They help us. How could you treat them like that?"

Jacques looked bewildered. "Why are you so upset, Mrs. Dean?" he said. "Heck, it happened on a Saturday. School was closed."

I couldn't help myself. I burst out laughing, even as part of me wanted to cry. After all we had done, after all the progress we had made, Jacques and his friends still thought it was all right to shoplift as long as the school was closed for the weekend.

When we dealt with one problematic aspect in the children's behaviour, another seemed to pop up to replace it. In spite of Jacques's transgression, shoplifting had begun to drop off significantly, when we heard reports of other unacceptable behaviour. Among the many businesses at the mall was a weight-loss clinic. The clinic's patrons, who were already conscious of their appearance and the need to reduce their weight, began complaining to the owner of remarks being directed at them from some of our students. "Pig!" and "Fat cow!" were just two of the comments made by the children as the customers arrived. This was so upsetting to the patrons, and so damaging to the clinic operator, that she began circulating a petition to have all South Simcoe students banished from the entire mall.

The incidents in front of the weight-loss clinic were not the only ones of their kind. Some South Simcoe kids were also verbally abusing visitors to the blood donor clinic in the mall.

We needed to do something quickly. One solution was to widen the Circles of Respect to include others in the local community. The Respect program was working well within the school; why couldn't it work as well beyond it? If kids have sufficient self-respect, compassion and sensitivity, I knew, they would see that hurling insults at innocent strangers was hurtful, unkind and disrespectful. But that would be a long-term goal. For the moment we needed to patch things up with the merchants, and save our promising program.

Once again I turned to Phil Lawson of Swiss Chalet and Peter Jefferson, the Kmart manager, for help. They quickly organized a meeting at the restaurant, inviting the mall merchants, our staff, and several parents as well. We needed Phil's natural diplomacy and his ability to see both sides of the debate, because many of the merchants arrived visibly angered. "Something has to be done about those kids," the manager of the weight-loss clinic almost shouted, thumping her fist on the table. "Something drastic. We cannot have them coming over here when they feel like it and shouting horrible things at our customers, scaring them away. They're stealing merchandise when our backs are turned, and generally acting as though they own the place."

Phil explained how his involvement with the school had changed things at Swiss Chalet. "Since I started working with the kids, I don't have problems anymore," he said. Then, his voice softened, he added: "They're just kids. We have to get together and help them." Phil's words were spoken with deep sincerity, and as he began to relate examples of the positive results he had observed, he began to win others over to his side.

"Maybe we can all find some way of working together and do something for the kids," one of the merchants offered. "If we can all work with the school, the kids will know we care about them and be more respectful to us," another suggested. "I mean the entire mall and the whole school."

"How about the Santa Claus parade?" It was the owner of the weight-loss clinic, the same woman who had earlier been so demanding of tougher discipline. The City of Oshawa sponsored an annual Santa Claus parade through the city to officially launch the holiday season. "Maybe we can enter a float in the parade, representing both the school and the mall," they suggested.

Almost everyone began nodding their heads at the idea. Everyone, that is, except me. I loved the enthusiasm being generated, and the fact that they wanted to do so much for the kids thrilled me. But I had always emphasized the concept of balance to my staff. Christmas was a stressful time for many, and the staff would be facing demands on their attention at home. I was afraid they were assuming too much responsibility—the parade was less than three weeks away, report cards were due, there was so much planning to be done...

Before I could voice my concerns, the idea took on a life of its own. With everyone contributing ideas, it was agreed that the South Simcoe float in the city's Santa Claus parade would be a joint production by the school and the mall. Everyone seemed enthusiastic and confident. "We can handle the workload," the staff members assured me when the meeting ended. "We really want to do it!"

For months I had been telling staff and students alike that they must have dreams and set goals, then be determined to make them real. How could I suggest they had taken on too much responsibility now? But I had serious reservations.

They were soon dispelled.

The husband of one of our staff members, an enthusiastic amateur pilot, managed to obtain some hangar space, where the float could be constructed, at the local airport. Every evening for two weeks the staff, mall merchants and members of the local Kiwanis Club pitched in to design and build a South Simcoe float, working in the unheated airplane hanger. That year the Oshawa Santa Claus parade featured a joint presentation from the mall and the school, with students waving and cheering from the back of a large flatbed truck—decorated with a giant banner declaring "Community Partnerships."

The meeting, which had been called to find ways of splitting the mall and school apart, actually produced a method of bringing them closer together than ever before, working in partnership for the education and well-being of the children.

As the number of our community partners grew, I was

careful to involve only those dedicated to giving openly and lovingly of their time. This attitude, and the actions reflecting it, meant so much more to the children than a simple expenditure of money. I wanted partners motivated not by a need to assuage their conscience or enhance their corporate image, but by a sense of social responsibility to help educate the children. People who wanted to work with us and agreed to abide by our guiding principles were much more important to us than those who simply offered to write us a cheque. Whenever we discussed working with a potential new community partner, our first question was: "What's in it for the children?" If the benefits to them were minimal, we either proposed a different kind of contribution or politely declined the offer.

Partners who contributed their time to help the children discovered wonderful, often unexpected, rewards. The kids at South Simcoe were not too "cool" to hide their appreciation for the partners' efforts. Their openly expressed joy made the partners feel needed and important, which in turn encouraged them to spend more time with the children and explore more ways of lending assistance. "The smiles on the faces of those kids when they see me," one man told me, "is something I have never experienced before. It keeps bringing me back."

Our remarkable success in reaching out beyond the school grounds encouraged me to introduce new programs to enhance the curriculum. One, called The Choice is Yours, brought successful people who had suffered difficult childhood experiences, similar to those faced by many South Simcoe kids, to the school as guest speakers. "Don't exaggerate and don't try to whitewash the things you went through," we advised the speakers. We explained that these were streetwise children with realistic views of the world. "Talk about the small decisions you made, the ones that made a difference," we suggested, adding: "Just be totally honest and totally upfront with the kids. They won't accept lies, and they don't need horror stories. They need to know that everyone has the power to make choices that can change their own lives, and they need assurance that they have the power to change their lives too."

Simply put, our kids needed inspiration. It may have been a difficult lesson to absorb, given their age and situation, but I wanted them to understand that, while adversity is not what we wish for, often our greatest growth occurs as a result of our trials. It was, I had to admit to myself, a lesson I too was learning. Personal stories, told by an adult who refused to let problems defeat him or her, helped the kids to understand that alternatives really did exist. A choice could be made after all—that would be the lesson.

The Choice is Yours demonstrated the various opportunities in life that are available to everyone who suffers serious home and personal problems. The seeds of our success are within all of us, if we search hard enough; that was the basic message.

One of the most popular The Choice is Yours speakers was Zanana Akande, minister of social services with the Ontario provincial government at the time. While the students may not have fully realized all of Zanana's responsibilities, they recognized that she played a vital role in managing many important affairs, so they were taken aback when she asked: "How many of you have to study in the bathroom because there is no other private place to read or do your school work?"

Most students in the audience raised their hands.

"Well, so did I," she said. "But I did not let it get me down or stand in my way, and you should not either."

They immediately warmed to Zanana and began to pepper her with all sorts of questions, even asking her age. When she told them, they gasped. Of course all children in their early teens assume that anyone over thirty is a dinosaur. In fact the next question was, "What kind of cream do you use on your face to keep your skin looking so young?" which sent the province's minister of social services erupting in gales of laughter.

She was still chuckling when she bid me goodbye at the end of her visit. "Here I was, ready to answer all kinds of questions about my work and the government and such," she giggled, "and some kid wants to know what kind of face cream I use. It just made my day!"

Zanana was so taken by the students, and they with her, that she invited them to visit her at her office in the provincial legislature a few weeks later.

Somehow, everyone seemed a little more casual and relaxed in the new atmosphere at South Simcoe. Later in our The Choice is Yours program, Richard Irish, a business partner from Investors Group, made it possible for Robert Esmie, the Olympic gold medallist, to visit our school. He came bouncing down the hall as though strolling on the beach and, spotting me standing near a doorway, sashayed up, gave me his broadest grin and said, "How you doin'? You smell sweet, girl."

"Thank you, and welcome to South Simcoe Public School," I replied. "You must be Robert Esmie. Allow me to introduce myself. I," I said in my mock-stern voice, "am the principal."

Robert quickly grew sober and apologetic, like one of our Grade Six boys who had been caught being naughty, until I convulsed in laughter.

His message to the students was similar to other speakers' in the program. Flashing his gold medal, won at the 1996 Atlanta Olympics, he told them that winning the medal was the fulfillment of a dream he had when he was their age, growing up in the rough Northern Ontario mining city of Sudbury. Robert and his friends all had dreams, and they shared them with each other. One boy wanted to become a doctor, another a teacher, and still another dreamed of becoming a karate master, opening his own school and maybe appearing in movies. Robert, of course, wanted to win a medal at the Olympics.

Here was the core of his story: *No one laughed at the others' dreams.* In fact they all promised to help one another achieve their dreams as they grew older, and they actually did. Even when some moved far from the city, the boys kept in touch, reminding each other of their dreams and how important they were. "And you know what?" Robert said. "We all made our dreams come true. We all became who we wanted to be. We never gave up."

The children sat enthralled. Here was an honest-to-goodness hero, describing all the hardships he had suffered as a young child, first growing up in Jamaica, where he had to share a bed with his two brothers, and later training steadily for days on end, often alone and with no promise of success, just to make his dream come true.

"You can become anything you want to be," Robert said, "from a sports hero to an A-average student. The important thing is to have a dream, treasure it, and do the things that will help make it real someday." People may scoff at your dream, he warned them. That doesn't matter. They had to keep believing in it, and believing in themselves. "Your biggest supporter," he said, "has to be you."

From others it might have sounded like just another pep talk, but Robert himself had put up with laughter from others about his dream. When he graduated from high school, Robert was a scrawny 115-pound kid who slept with a relay baton in his hand every night so it would become as much a part of him as his own hand, and so he could fall asleep dreaming of running the perfect relay race. "I began working out to build my muscles," he told the children, "and kept finding ways to run faster. And here I am today." Then he displayed the same baton his relay team had carried to win the Olympic gold medal. "And here is the baton I used." Nobody, of course, was laughing at Robert now.

He didn't sugar-coat life for the South Simcoe kids. He knew some of the hurdles these kids would face, because he had encountered some himself. They were bound to face temptations, like drugs, that would pull them away from their dreams. They had to recognize these temptations for what they were: barriers to making their dreams come true. They had to use all the problems they encountered, and overcame, to make themselves stronger. "Don't ever forget where you are coming from," he advised them, "and always know where you are going."

Later he let every child handle his precious Olympic gold medal. "Make a wish when you touch it," he suggested, and I will never forget the expressions on their faces as they closed their eyes, made their wish and imagined their dream coming true in the presence of a real-life hero.

Another speaker demonstrated the strong awareness children retained of major issues and of the world beyond their own community. Roland Hosein, a vice-president of General Electric Canada whose responsibilities included managing the company's environmental health and safety, made several valuable contributions to our work and, naturally, I invited him to take part in a session of The Choice is Yours. As soon as the children learned that he dealt with environmental issues, they began grilling him about his company's commitment to recycling materials and reducing pollution. Intrigued by technological advances in environmental matters, they surprised and impressed the GE executive with their awareness of issues and their leading-edge ideas, such as launching an inter-scholastic Internet-based dialogue on environmental issues, and GE became another valued community partner.

My friend Lucy Greene, whose company had provided us with new furnishings when we so desperately needed them, also arrived as part of our The Choice is Yours program. Born into an immigrant Ukrainian family and now the mother of six children, Lucy had earned her MBA while in her mid-forties and risen to a top executive position with a giant corporation. "And you know what?" she told the children when they were suitably impressed. "I couldn't even speak English when I started school. Not a word!" Like many immigrant families, Lucy's had emphasized over and over again the importance of obtaining an education, and Lucy had taken it to heart.

"It's not just a matter of working to improve your math or your reading scores," Lucy advised them. "Focus on making the choice to get better and better. Just keep trying to improve. Never, never give up. You can do it, but you have to make the choice."

Some of the senior students were so taken by Lucy that they accepted her invitation to visit her at her office, high in a gleaming skyscraper in midtown Toronto. For many of them this was their first visit to the big city, and I'm sure they were quietly amazed that this warm woman, who had achieved so much success in her career, knew not a word of English as a young schoolgirl.

Many more participants in our program arrived at South Simcoe Public School. Some were not as colourful or mesmerizing as Lucy, Robert and Zanana, but each provided the children with a sense of the world beyond their neighbourhood, and the realization that others had overcome hardships similar to those being endured by the students of South Simcoe.

Chapter 7

The Limits of Love

Many people who ask me about South Simcoe seem to focus on the challenge of supervising the students and managing their behaviour. This was, in fact, a major concern for us at the beginning, and naturally a primary responsibility for me as principal. Many of the challenges were directly linked to problems of vandalism, schoolyard bullying, temper tantrums, aggression and anger. "But these are not the causes of problems," I want to say to my questioners. "They are the *results* of deeply rooted problems." I have never believed in merely treating problems as they occur. I prefer to get at the root of problems and take steps to prevent them happening again.

More to the point: the headaches caused by the many "problem children" we encountered over the years were offset by their response to our efforts to meet their need for respect, affection, attention and, yes, love. Sometimes the reaction of the children set us laughing in unbridled joy. And sometimes the tragedy of their lives sent us off into a dark corner to weep in despair.

Here are just a few of the many children in need of love and caring we encountered at South Simcoe—the ones that still flood our memory with joy, sadness and hope, and sometimes a twinge of regret.

We all suffer setbacks, injustice and pain in our lives. As adults we learn to accept and deal with it. But children are not equipped to handle unfairness without severe emotional scarring and distress, and no one was more injured this way than Maria.

Maria had so many strikes against her that it seemed difficult, at first, to imagine that her life could become even more tragic. But it did.

Her life was a nightmare. Besides watching her family struggle through unemployment and poverty, Maria had to endure the dual challenge of dealing with both a learning problem and being hearing impaired. She had been given a hearing aid to wear, but it embarrassed her, and she often removed the device, trying to get through classes without fully understanding all that was being said to her. To compound things, she wore the aid to some classes and not to others, so not all her teachers knew of her disability.

All children are beautiful in their own special way, but Maria was even challenged in this respect. Her brown hair was long and stringy, and her eyes bore constant dark circles and a perpetually lost look. On the rare occasions when she smiled, it was a bittersweet expression, like an attempt to conceal some hidden adversity. She also dressed in baggy, hand-me-down clothes that added to the image of destitution.

There was more. Although she had advanced to Grade Nine, Maria's progress was so poor that, at her own request after consulting with a social worker and her high school principal, she was admitted to Grade Eight in South Simcoe.

It made good sense, because Maria would receive the special attention she needed at our smaller school. But the blow to her already crippled self-esteem must have been devastating.

My first sight of Maria, looking so lost and forlorn, made me determined to help her succeed. We accommodated her hearing impairment in various ways, and assured her that we would do all we could to help her return to high school the following year. With luck and hard work she would taste success after all, and we were pleased when she began to respond with better grades.

Then we discovered she was pregnant. As a result of a rape.

Her attacker, Maria told us, had crept up behind her when she wasn't wearing her hearing aid. She did not hear him coming and, when it was over, refused to tell anyone about it. For months she hid her condition beneath her baggy clothing until it became too obvious.

I managed to avoid crying about Maria until I arrived home that evening, and then I let the floodgates open. Maria was barely into her teens, bedevilled by problems many adults would have difficulty coping with, and now this: a child having a baby. What more could happen to her?

I discovered the answer a few days later.

One of Maria's friends, seeking to raise her spirits, loaned her a necklace to wear. During the lunch hour Maria was in the shopping mall across the street from the school when she encountered her friend's mother, a woman who knew of Maria's troubles and condition. Unfairly, the woman assumed that Maria had stolen the necklace from her daughter, and she attacked Maria, physically and verbally, in front of other students and several mall shoppers.

"You thieving little bitch!" she screamed, as Maria cowered against a wall. The mother demanded the necklace back, in spite of Maria's tearful explanation. "The only thing that's any good about you is what you have between your legs!" the mother shouted with unspeakable cruelty. "At least you can trade it for favours. Otherwise, there's nothing good about you, and there never will be, you little tramp!" Strangers stopped and stared, some with contempt, others with disapproval, all of it directed at Maria.

Maria returned to school in near hysteria, feeling more shame than anyone should be asked to bear. She poured her little heart out in my office between sobs. She had done nothing wrong. She was not a bad girl. Why, then, was all this happening to her?

I comforted her as much as I could and promised to invite the mother in for a chat and an explanation.

Even when the mother learned the truth, she refused to offer an apology. "She shouldn't have been wearing my daughter's necklace," was her best explanation.

After she left, I sat wondering about a woman who would value a piece of cheap jewellery over the feelings of another human being. What kinds of values was she teaching her own children? What kinds of scars would they bear through life as a result?

Maria had her child in May. The following month she appeared back at the school, her month-old baby daughter in her arms and determined to write her final exams. Maria's mother, she informed us, was unable to babysit the child that day. This posed a major dilemma for me. The presence of a month-old baby in the examination room was certain to be at least distracting to the other students. But I was impressed with Maria's resolve, and she obviously sensed my concern. "Don't worry," she assured me. "She's just been fed, so she'll be all right for an hour or so."

We could hardly refuse her. "I knew you guys would help me!" Maria grinned when we agreed to the idea. Kim watched over the little one while her mother wrote her Grade Eight final examination, and when some of the children finished their exams early, they volunteered to remain in the school, taking care of the baby in Kim's place. If I had had any doubts about our success at creating a true family atmosphere at South Simcoe, they were surely dispelled that day.

As educators, we accept that marriage breakdowns, economic disasters, parental addiction problems and a host of other factors may seem to counterbalance our efforts in the classroom. Even though these kinds of events threaten to overwhelm everything we're trying to achieve with the children, we must continue helping them to develop an inner strength and self-confidence. In this way, they may become more resilient and better able to face the various challenges of life.

Leonard arrived at South Simcoe from Edmonton, enrolling in Grade Six during mid-term. An attractive, fair-haired boy with pleasant manners, Leonard seemed to fit in quickly. He made friends easily and his school work was adequate, if not spectacular.

Rather quickly, however, the staff and I noticed his strange, unpredictable behaviour. "Sometimes when I'm talking to Leonard," his teacher told me, "he just isn't here. He's off somewhere, in a world of his own, and he doesn't hear a word you say."

I suggested to her that daydreaming was hardly unheard of among children of Leonard's age.

"This is more than daydreaming," she replied. "When I finally get his attention, sometimes he gets right to work and other times he explodes in anger. He'll swear and shout, or throw a book across the room. He becomes very frightening, and then settles down almost as fast. It's as though he has two personalities, one sweet and the other scary."

It sounded as if Leonard was suffering from a serious psychological problem, so we made inquiries at his previous school in Edmonton. Had they any record of similar behaviour during Leonard's years there? No, the answer came back, he had been considered a pleasant, well-behaved youngster.

I grew curious and concerned. Something had happened to change this boy's personality. Relocation is almost always difficult for an eleven-year-old, but Leonard's reaction seemed extreme.

I discovered that Leonard was living with his maternal grandparents in Oshawa, and I contacted them to chat about Leonard and his problem. Bit by bit, the causes of Leonard's behaviour became clear.

Leonard had arrived at South Simcoe in a state of shock. Back in Edmonton his mother, a single parent, had died suddenly. This was traumatic enough for any young boy, but the death had not been accidental. She had been murdered. As if that weren't enough, Leonard learned through extensive media coverage of his mother's death that she had been a prostitute, slain on the street where she worked. Leonard had loved his mother deeply and had no inkling that her evening "job" consisted of meeting strange men and letting them take her to hotel rooms for sex.

It wasn't just Leonard who discovered the truth about his mother, of course. His Edmonton schoolmates learned it as well and, as children will, began to tease him about it. When the pain became too much for Leonard to bear, a decision was made to send him east to live with his still-grieving grandparents. Leonard may have left the taunts of his school chums back in Edmonton, but he carried all his agony to South Simcoe with him. Knowing the cause of his suffering helped us to understand Leonard's extreme behaviour. Nevertheless, there was worse to come.

One Monday morning, two boys about Leonard's age approached me in the hall. "Can we talk to you about Leonard?" they asked me. They appeared concerned, almost frightened.

Curious, I invited them into my office, where they stumbled over themselves to describe what had taken place over the weekend.

Leonard, it seemed, had invited the boys to his grandparents' house for a visit. "Do you want to meet my mom?" Leonard asked them at one point. Before they could reply, Leonard removed a ceramic urn from the shelf, carried it to them and lifted the lid. Inside were the ashes of Leonard's cremated mother. "Here," Leonard said, handing one of the boys the urn. "That's my mother. Say hello to her."

When the boys pulled away in shock and horror, the urn almost slipped from Leonard's hands. But it was his friend's words that sent Leonard over the edge.

"Man, you're weird," the boy said. "You're totally nuts! What's wrong with you, anyway?"

"Are you going to hold her?" Leonard demanded. "Are you going to hold my mother or not?"

"No, I'm not!" the boy replied. He and Leonard's other friend looked disgusted.

Leonard set the urn aside, left the room and quickly

returned carrying his grandfather's shotgun. "You hold the urn or you get out of my house," Leonard screamed, aiming the weapon at them. Naturally, they fled in terror.

"You have to do something about him," one of the boys said to me. "He's crazy!"

I was glad I had taken the time to discover something of Leonard's background. Leonard was not crazy. Hurt, confused, angry and unloved perhaps; but not crazy. Of course, once the boys spread the story about Leonard's threat with the shotgun among other students, Leonard became more alone than ever.

Beyond providing as much understanding as we could, we knew we had to obtain counselling for Leonard. The experience also provided us with a "teachable moment," an opportunity to help our students understand the pain other members are experiencing, and how compassion is needed at times like this.

Leonard became entangled in a custody battle and was returned to Edmonton shortly after the episode with the shotgun. We provided his new school with as much background information about Leonard as we could, and hoped he would receive the assistance he so desperately needed.

Leonard is out there somewhere, trying to deal with all his pain and anger. We just hope he is not dealing with it alone.

Cathy's case was similar to Leonard's in some ways. Cathy was the picture of innocence: large, bright blue eyes, silky shoulder-length hair, and a mobile face that could change from deep, serious thought into a mischievous grin at the speed of light. I enjoyed speaking to her and seeing the glow of her smile appear, like rays of sun breaking through a cloudy sky. I loved hearing her read aloud in class, watching her beam with pride at her accomplishments, which were well above the level of most of her classmates.

One morning when Cathy failed to appear for her Grade One class, we followed normal procedures for our "Safe Arrival" system and called home to confirm the mother's knowledge of her absence. The woman's response sent waves of fear rolling through everyone. "What do you mean she's not at school?" she said, her voice already shaking. "I took her there myself this morning. I watched her walk into the schoolyard and we waved goodbye to each other. *What do you mean she's not there now??!!*"

While waiting for Cathy's mother to arrive at the school, we asked other students in her class if they had seen Cathy arrive. One had, and her story was chilling. According to this little girl's account, Cathy had been in the playground before entering the school building when a man appeared out of nowhere and carried her off. Fearing the worst, we began interviewing students in their classrooms, asking if anyone had witnessed Cathy's abduction. Two Grade Eight students had and, streetwise as they were, they provided a detailed description of the man.

"He didn't look so strange," one of them said. "I mean, he had tattoos and long hair, and he was wearing a black leather jacket."

"He called her name, and she ran up to him and they hugged each other," the other student added. "Then he picked her up and carried her off. She wasn't kicking or screaming or anything."

"If she had," his friend said, "we would have said something or stopped him ourselves. We just thought he was her dad."

The teachers on yard supervision that morning had not

noticed anything unusual. My fear, of course, was that the tattooed man may have taken time to learn Cathy's name and build her trust, so he could abduct her without causing a scene. I immediately called the police to report the incident and was still talking to one of the officers when a woman we understood to be Cathy's mother arrived, near hysterics.

When she heard the students' description of the man seen with Cathy, and the police added that they had received reports of a suspicious man in the neighbourhood, the mother held her head in her hands. "It's Phil," she said. "Oh my God, it must be Phil."

The police asked who Phil was.

"Her father," she replied. "He must have gotten out of jail."

When I asked the woman who had custody and what rights she had regarding Cathy's care, she sobbed, "I don't have any rights."

Slowly, the full story emerged.

When Arlene, the woman who called herself Cathy's mother, first met Phil, he was caring for Cathy, who was just six months old at the time. Cathy's mother had been sent to prison on serious criminal charges, and Arlene and Phil soon began a common-law relationship. But Phil became involved in serious trouble with the law as well. During one of his infrequent times out of jail, Phil assaulted Arlene, frightening her so much that she moved out of the home they had shared, taking Cathy with her. She had to; without Arlene, Cathy had nowhere else to go. Besides, Cathy considered Arlene to be her actual mother, and Arlene loved Cathy as though the girl were her own flesh and blood. By all reports Arlene was a caring mother, doing as well as she could under the circumstances.

Convicted of trafficking in cocaine, Phil had spent much

of the past four years in prison. Now it appeared he had reclaimed his daughter and carried her away, for reasons we did not understand, to a place we did not know.

"Would he hurt the child?" a police officer asked Arlene.

She shook her head. She didn't think so. In fact, she suggested, Phil had probably taken Cathy because, as her parent, he thought that he would qualify to receive welfare payments.

The police were naturally concerned, but they were a little confused as well. The father had not actually kidnapped the child; he had legal custody, after all. They were just about to leave the school, promising to look for Phil and Cathy, when my telephone rang. It was Phil. I waved the police back into my office while demanding to know if Phil still had Cathy with him. He assured me he had, and that she was fine.

I could barely restrain my anger. "You could have had the courtesy to come into the school and explain who you were and what you were doing," I told him. "The police are here. We have been looking for the child, assuming she had been kidnapped."

His lame explanation was that he doubted the school would have released Cathy into his care. In that respect he may have been correct, of course.

I handed the telephone to the police, who took down all the details of Phil and Cathy's whereabouts, and his plans for her. Phil planned to return home to Toronto, taking Cathy with him. She would be out of the school, out of our lives and, tragically, out of the life of Arlene, who had unselfishly loved and cared for the little girl for much of her life.

It didn't end there.

Arlene remained in my office, where she spent much of the day grieving for Cathy, spinning us stories of Cathy as she grew into a trusting and loving child. I suggested Arlene might be able to obtain legal advice based on her role as Cathy's surrogate mother, and I asked her to stay in touch with the school and keep us informed. When I called Arlene a few days later, she told me in a still-tearful voice that a legal-aid lawyer thought she had only a slim chance of winning custody, and in any event it would require a long and probably bitter court battle. I assured her that we were there if she needed us.

Later, when I realized we had not heard from Arlene for some time, I dialled the telephone number she had left with us. The woman who answered explained that Arlene had moved away. No, Arlene had left no forwarding address and the woman had no idea where Arlene had gone. We never heard from Arlene again.

But we did hear from Cathy.

One day I received a telephone call from the principal of a public school in one of the western provinces. Cathy, the principal said, was a difficult child. She refused to speak a word to anyone—not to other students, not to the teachers. She had become very withdrawn. It had taken quite a while to track us down, and the principal was looking for some guidance in helping her come out of her shell. Cathy's father, Phil, the principal informed me, was back in jail, and the little girl was back in the care of a new girlfriend.

My heart almost shattered at the news. Was this really our bright, precocious Cathy, the little girl who giggled at funny stories during reading time and sometimes skipped hand in hand across the playground with her friends? I quickly outlined her situation to the principal, then suggested she hand the receiver to Cathy. Perhaps she would speak to me.

When I heard her small voice say hello, I answered, "Hi,

Cathy. This is Mrs. Dean from South Simcoe. Do you remember me?"

Indeed she did. "Mrs. Dean," she pleaded. "Will you come and get me, please?" She began to cry.

My eyes filled with tears. Summoning all my training to keep my voice calm, I told Cathy that we all missed her, and we wanted to know how she was doing. Through her tears Cathy assured me she was doing fine.

"I just spoke to your principal," I said. "She seems like a very nice lady, and she likes you very much. So will you show her your very best work? And will you read to her from your book, the way you used to read to me?"

Across all the miles of telephone wires, I heard her small voice promise, "Yes."

"Your principal will let you call here if you need to talk to us," I said, and we talked for a little while longer before saying goodbye. Hanging up the phone, I sat for several minutes reflecting on all the trust that children place in adults, and consoling myself that Cathy was in the hands of a caring colleague.

Every teacher's experience is a microcosm of life. But events of joy and sadness, triumph and tragedy, victory and loss just seemed to be drawn with sharper edges—literally, in one terrifying case—at South Simcoe.

Where children such as Cathy could melt your heart with one unexpected smile, Tom could harden your resolve with a single angry glance. Tom, a Grade Eight student, practically snarled his way through every day at school, terrifying the children and insulting the teachers. The various strategies we tried were apparently not very effective, and when he made a particularly vicious comment to his teacher,

Anne, in class one day, I called him into my office for a one-on-one session.

I began by telling him his behaviour was totally unacceptable.

Tom claimed he had done nothing wrong.

"Let's be honest here," I said firmly. "Is that the way you should be speaking to your teacher?"

"Why not?" he shrugged. "She hates me," he said.

"She does not hate you." This teacher was as dedicated to her students as anyone in the school. "She loves her class. She cares about all her students."

"Yeah?" Tom sneered. "Well, she hates me. That's why I bug the hell out of her."

I called Anne and asked her to join us. "Tom is convinced that you hate him," I told her, meeting her alone outside my office. "That's why he is so obnoxious in the classroom."

Anne sighed, and shook her head. "You know what, Sandra?" she said. "I hadn't thought about it before, but I really do dislike that kid. I'm trying not to dislike him, but his behaviour is driving me crazy."

Although Anne tried to conceal her feelings towards Tom, he was able to sense them. Anne continuously complimented Tom on his appearance and congratulated him on the way he had begun a project, even when he failed to complete it. When she brought treats to the entire class, Anne personally ensured that Tom received one, and whenever she spoke to Tom she placed her hand on his shoulder as a gesture of affection. But nothing seemed to reach the boy. Perhaps, I suggested, we could work together to find something about Tom that she could relate to, some aspect of his personality she could find appealing. Then we could build on that. (I was, of course, harking back to my mother's lesson to me about the Christmas doll.) What if we invited Tom's mother to the school? All four of us could discuss the problem, and perhaps a solution would reveal itself.

Anne was skeptical, fearing that Tom would continue his rudeness, but I persuaded her to join them in a meeting in my office. "Meanwhile," I suggested, "try complimenting Tom when he deserves it. Maybe he'll change his attitude towards you."

Tom's mother arrived the following week. She was a pleasant woman, but somewhat guarded at first. The most remarkable thing I noticed was the change that his mother's presence made in Tom's personality. The tyrant of South Simcoe Public School had been transformed into a submissive little angel, sitting silently next to his mother and beaming with joy whenever she gave him a smile.

Anne and I were both amazed, especially when Anne revealed all the ways in which she had tried to persuade Tom that she and the rest of the staff indeed loved him—or were trying to.

"I don't dislike Tom," Anne told the mother. "I honestly want him to do well. But he can be very frustrating. He simply does not respond to me."

"He gives everybody a hard time at first," Tom's mother said. "It's his way of testing you, to see if you really like him or not. The trouble is," she admitted, "he usually gives people such a hard time that they're turned off him."

I was amazed that the mother would admit this so openly. To her credit, the mother promised to work with us and try to change Tom's belligerent attitude. I couldn't persuade her to join us at Parent Rap, where I felt we might make real progress, but both Anne and I noticed a change in Tom once his mother became seriously involved and began signing the

Tracking Sheets and returning phone calls. Eventually, Tom and Anne got along very well together, showing respect for each other.

Tom remained one of the toughest kids in school, which made a subsequent incident with Ted all the more frightening. If Tom could be frightened by something, or someone, it had to be serious. And it was.

It was Ted.

Ted had been at South Simcoe barely a month. We knew he would be a handful; Ted brought a history of violence with him and, as a matter of fact, had been arrested and charged with assault. We also knew that Ted's home life was somewhat chaotic. Ted transferred to us after he moved out of his father's home and into a home shared by his mother and new stepfather. Large for his age, with long dark hair and narrow eyes that seemed always to be filled with suspicion, even Ted's clothes appeared chosen to intimidate others. By dressing in heavy flannel shirts, worn jeans and heavy work boots, he looked more like a construction worker than a Grade Eight student.

One day, just before afternoon classes began, Tom arrived at my office door, clearly frightened. This in itself was disturbing; nothing seemed to scare Tom, or so he wanted everyone to believe. But Ted had threatened Tom with a knife during the lunch hour, a threat serious enough for Tom to report it. Sending Tom back to his class, I called Ted to my office, sat him down in a chair, then quietly asked my secretary to call Ted's home and request his parents to come to the school.

Ted was sprawled across the chair, his entire body a sneer.

"You're new here, Ted," I began, "and we haven't had

time to get to know each other yet." I seated myself across from him. "I have a problem that I need you to help me with."

No response.

"Is it true you have a knife?" I asked. "There are reports that you have brought a knife to school."

Ted mumbled that he didn't have a knife.

I stood up. "Where is the knife?" I asked.

"Maybe I have a knife," he said with a slight smile. "Maybe it's in my locker and maybe it's in my pocket."

"I want to know where the knife is, Ted," I said. "You are not allowed to have a knife in the school. Besides, you are threatening some of the children with it. That is simply unacceptable. I want you to tell me where the knife is."

The smile became a snicker. "Maybe it's in my locker," he said. His hands were in his pockets. "Or maybe it's right here in my hand."

I made a quick decision, keeping in mind the safety of the other children, and called to my secretary, Joan. "We have a situation here," I said. That was her cue to call the police. Then I turned back to Ted.

"Ted," I said firmly, "you can give the knife to me now or you can give it to the police."

He gave it to me. He withdrew one of the ugliest, most fearsome knives I had ever seen from his pocket, holding it not like he was about to hand it to me but as though he was prepared to use it as a weapon. When I finally took my eyes from the knife, I saw Ted staring at me in the strange hooded way he had, his mouth set in an expression somewhere between anger and determination. Too late, I realized that I should have waited for the police to handle the matter, instead of demanding the knife from him myself. In one quick motion, I knew, Ted could thrust the blade into my body from where he sat.

"That's some knife," I said, trying to keep my voice calm.

"Yeah," he answered in a voice that sounded like it belonged to someone ten years older. "It's to kill anybody that bothers me," he said. "And I'm keeping it." Then he slowly curled into his chair, one hand still pointing the knife in my direction, the other hand a clenched fist, the knuckles white. His eyes began darting here and there and his body continued to fold into itself, like a coiled spring under constant tension.

OK, I said to myself, this is not just a case of childish bravado on his part. Ted is already facing two criminal charges, and he could easily overpower you if he chose to.

I had no way of handling the situation except through my words, and I continued speaking, keeping my voice low and my words gentle. I assured Ted that I would not try to take the knife away from him.

At that moment, Ted's stepfather arrived.

A tall, casually dressed man who also happened to be an ex–police officer, the stepfather took in the situation at a glance but made no comment as he sat down on the other side of the boy. He and I introduced ourselves as though everything were normal, and I explained that Ted did not want to give up his knife. Meanwhile, Ted remained curled in the same position, the knife still clutched in his hand, with a new hint of fear in his eyes.

"I asked if he had a knife," I said to the stepfather. "Since you're here now, perhaps you can explain the problem to Ted. Ted says that he needs it for protection, but it's against the rules to have a knife in school."

Thankfully, Ted's stepfather kept his voice as low and

controlled as my own. "Ted," he said, "hand me the knife. You've heard Mrs. Dean say that you're not supposed to have it at school. You've already said you don't intend to use it on anyone. So why not give me the knife?"

Ted's response was to curl even tighter into his coiled-spring posture. I was afraid things might actually become worse until the stepfather added, "You won't be in any more trouble if you give me the knife." He turned to me. "Is that right, Mrs. Dean?"

I assured him he was correct, adding that a suspension would be necessary. "Perhaps Ted wasn't aware of the rule against bringing knives to school," I added. "If so, I'll take his word for it."

The tension slowly began to ease. The stepfather continued speaking in a calm, soothing voice until Ted finally handed the knife over to him.

I breathed a long sigh of relief, and the stepfather suggested that he and Ted should go home and have a serious talk together. By that time the police had arrived to take over the situation.

We had to suspend Ted over this incident, but he needed more than discipline. He needed the kind of specialized help we were unable to provide, and we had to accept the frustrating fact that we could never solve all the problems that arose within the walls of the school, no matter how hard we tried.

In some ways Ted was fortunate, I suppose. His stepfather not only cared about the boy but was a sensible and compassionate man with the ability to deal with Ted in a calm, effective manner. It is ironic that other children, who were more likeable and promising than Ted, often had to cope with parents lacking in those qualities. What's more, these same children often became protective of their parents to a surprising degree, as though they were saying, "I know they have their faults, but they are my parents and I love them anyway."

Nothing illustrated this better than my experience with nine-year-old Bobby during one of our periodic attacks on head lice. This, by the way, is not strictly an inner-city-school phenomenon. Head-lice infestations in children can, and do, occur in the most respectable of suburban schools.

In any case, parents of children with head lice were instructed to treat the problem with special shampoo and to remove the eggs by combing the child's hair thoroughly before sending him or her back to school. Some children returned with their heads still infested with eggs. We contacted the parents about the problem, and when many said they lacked the money to purchase shampoo, Joan and I arranged to purchase some, at wholesale cost, from the neighbouring Kmart store.

In addition to asking parents to perform regular checks at home, we followed the practice of many other schools and began to inspect for lice each term. This angered some parents enough that they phoned the school to complain, stating their children were clean and well groomed, and we had no right to inspect their hair. We discussed this at a Parent Rap session, explaining that head lice were not a sign of uncleanliness, just an unfortunate fact of life. Gradually we won all the parents over by inviting those who protested most vigorously to volunteer their assistance during scheduled head-lice inspections. Soon the inspections became another accepted part of our routine at South Simcoe, and another demonstration of the importance of parental involvement in decisions such as this.

Bobby was among the ones sent home for this treatment. He returned with lice still literally crawling through his hair. At first he assured us that his mother had performed the treatment. Later he admitted that he had lied. Once again we sent the boy home, this time with some shampoo to be used on his hair. We also called his mother to explain that we could not admit her son back into the classroom until the lice were treated.

Bobby was back at school the following day. Unfortunately, so were the lice.

We repeated the procedure of handing Bobby the shampoo, calling his mother and informing her of the need to treat Bobby's hair before he could be readmitted to class. She gave her assurance, Bobby went home, and he returned the next day with his hair as badly infested as ever.

I could not understand what was happening. Bobby knew the rules and his mother acknowledged the need, yet nothing was being done to treat the problem. Just to compound my confusion, Bobby's younger sister, Jennifer, who naturally shared the same lice problem, had returned with her hair shampooed, combed out and shiny from the very first day. How could one sibling's problem have been solved and another's ignored?

I called Bobby into my office, determined to get to the bottom of the mystery. After several gentle questions from me, Bobby began to cry. I asked him what was wrong.

Through his sobs he explained that his mother was often drunk when he asked her to shampoo his hair. "She doesn't like to do it," he said. "She just yanks at my hair and hurts me, and then she gives up." This was coming from one of the sweetest, most adorable and conscientious children in the school, and again I felt my heart break a little.

"Wait a moment," I said as he calmed down. "What about your sister Jennie? Her hair was done right the first time. Didn't your mother wash Jennie's hair?"

"No," Bobby said, shaking his head. "I did."

You might almost expect a child like this to grow resentful of his mother, angry that she could not fulfill this simple task for her son. But Bobby did not. During the session in my office Bobby admitted that he helped plan and prepare the family meals, sounding more like a concerned father and husband than a nine-year-old boy. Over and over he tried to convince me that his mother was wonderful in many ways, except that she had a drinking problem. "When she's drinking," he said, "she just can't do some things for us, and I don't know how to do them by myself." In spite of it all, Bobby still loved his mother. I had to understand that, and in a small way I did.

"Listen," I said. "What if I shampooed your hair myself, here in the school? Do you think your mother would mind?"

Bobby thought it would be fine with her, so I fetched the shampoo, walked with Bobby to the sink, rolled up my sleeves and went to work.

A few days later Jacki asked if I had noticed Bobby's hair.

"Don't tell me he has lice again," I said.

It wasn't lice. Bobby's hair was falling out. He already had a bald spot. An examination by the nurse indicated that Bobby was probably losing his hair as a result of stress, all of it based on his home life. One morning, Bobby's five-year-old sister arrived at school looking forlorn and wearing a heavy parka with the hood covering her head. Inside the school, she refused to remove the parka or even lower the hood. When her teacher finally persuaded her, she discovered that the mother's boyfriend and one of his buddies, hearing about the head-lice problem suffered by the children, decided to shave the little girl's hair off. She was now completely bald and embarrassed. We, of course, were furious. I felt compelled to report the situation to the Children's Aid Society, who had been monitoring the family for some time, and they began arranging to place Bobby and his sister with a foster family.

Bobby was devastated. When he discovered the news, he came running to me, convinced that I was responsible for breaking up his family. In a way I was, I suppose, but I felt as though I had betrayed a confidence with him.

"We all have a duty," I tried to explain, "and my duty is to make sure all the children in the school are cared for." His mother loved him, I was certain, but at the moment she was unable to provide all the care Bobby and his sister needed. Until she could provide it, Bobby and Jennifer needed help. "There is something else," I added. "The law tells us that we have to report things like this to the right people, who will find some way to help. If we don't do it, we would be breaking the law."

I think the idea of a school principal being in trouble with the law impressed Bobby, because he nodded glumly and said he understood. But he still wasn't happy. Neither, of course, were we.

Bobby and Jennie were assigned to a foster family in what seemed to be an ideal situation. They lived in a large, comfortable farmhouse with plenty to eat, animals to feed and care for, and adults who treated them with love and respect. But the parental bond is strong, so strong that both children constantly mourned the separation from their mother. And their mother too, when she was sober, grieved for them, calling them on the telephone and crying together with her children.

After a year the mother was persuasive enough to win Bobby and Jennie back to her home. Her drinking problem, she promised, was under control, and the children would be enrolled in South Simcoe once again. Soon after Bobby and Jennie returned to school, looking healthier and happier than I had ever seen them, I met with the mother in my office. My biggest fear, of course, was that the children would find themselves in the same intolerable situation as before, and I suppose my concern was visible to the mother.

"I know what you're thinking," she said. "You're thinking I won't take care of them the way I'm supposed to. Everybody is thinking that way. But they don't understand how much I missed those kids. I missed them a lot, and I'm trying my best to be a good mother."

I grew to like this woman. She was brusque and a little rough around the edges, but so were many people in the South Simcoe neighbourhood. The most important thing, I kept telling myself, was that she loved her children and they undoubtedly loved her, regardless of her failings. They were all going to try to make things better, and who was I to judge her?

But I began to suspect that the mother was sliding back into her old ways. There was nothing specific, just the feeling that the children were enduring the same old problems at home, but with a difference.

In the past the children had confided in us, and we could assure them that we understood and cared. Now they were secretive about their home life, afraid that once again the CAS would become involved and the family would be separated if the truth about their lives were revealed. In spite of her faults, the children preferred to be with their mother in their small house rather than on a large farm among caring strangers. Our attempt to improve their situation had cost us the children's trust and confidence.

Time and again, during those years at South Simcoe, we discovered the enormity of the problems faced by many of our children. As adults we learn to cope with these complications, and most of us have the ability to address them in one way or another. Children lack both the ability and the power to change their environment in a similar manner. They remain at the mercy of adult decisions, made in adult situations, and they are expected to accept them, often paying a high price in happiness and emotional stability. Nothing demonstrated this to us with greater impact or poignancy than Stephanie's rebellion, just prior to Christmas.

Stephanie had been transferred from a suburban Toronto school into Grade Eight in late October. She always dressed in expensive clothes, which made her conspicuous among most of the other students. During her first two or three months with us she appeared quiet and withdrawn, but otherwise co-operative.

One day in mid-December I entered my office to find Stephanie, visibly angry and sullen. All the students knew that my office was a refuge where they could cool off when their anger and frustration became too much to handle. Stephanie, I learned, had exploded in an outburst of anger, and directed her rage at her teacher, Doug. This surprised me, because Doug was noted for his patience and gentle manner. The cause of her outburst? A Christmas decorating activity, something the children usually looked forward to. Stephanie, however, called the work stupid and flatly refused to do it.

When Stephanie refused to discuss the situation with me,

I busied myself with work to give her time. Finally, I asked how she was doing.

"Not so good," she replied.

Stephanie seemed in no hurry to return to class, and I filed that away as I encouraged her to talk with me. Why, I asked, had she been so rude to Doug, who was a caring person trying to help her?

"He wants me to do some stupid Christmas thing for us to take home to our parents," she spat out. "And I don't want to do it. I don't want to have anything to do with Christmas, and I tried to tell him that, but he kept pushing and pushing . . . "

I realized immediately that Stephanie's anger had nothing to do with the art activity. "You don't like Christmas?" I asked.

She hated it. "All you people keep talking about is Christmas, Christmas, Christmas. I'm sick of it. Don't you guys understand this will be the worst Christmas of my life?"

I told her no, I didn't understand. Then I came around from my desk and settled next to her. "Help me understand, Stephanie," I said.

It was like opening a door to a storehouse of anger, sadness and tragedy.

She began by asking if I knew how much it cost to celebrate Christmas. The gifts, the food, the decorations—you couldn't buy them without money, she reminded me. "I don't know what I'll even eat at Christmas," Stephanie said. "Maybe a sandwich, if I'm lucky. There'll be no presents, no tree, no turkey, nothing. My mother can't afford to do anything this year. Don't you realize what happened to me and my family?" she demanded. "We don't know what's going to happen to us, and you guys are running around the school singing and laughing and making decorations, and nobody knows what it's like in my home."

That's when the flood began. I put my arms around her while she sobbed and sobbed. "You know what, Mrs. Dean?" Stephanie said between sobs. "I might be dead this Christmas. I can't take this anymore. I can't!"

Her words sent a chill through me. The threat of suicide from an adolescent cannot be ignored. At the very least, it is a cry for help.

"I'm puzzled," I said to her. "You're always so well dressed, and your mother has a job. Maybe you're not rich, but I'm still confused over your concern about Christmas and money."

Then I listened.

Stephanie explained that she was well dressed because the clothes she wore had been purchased when she lived in a comfortable area of Toronto. Back then, both of Stephanie's parents had professional careers, earning good salaries. The family had owned two cars, lived well and took vacations, and life was stable and solidly middle class—until her father lost his job. There must have been some underlying financial or other problems, because when the father's search for work extended into weeks, and eventually months, the family was plunged into financial crisis. First they lost their cars, then they lost their house, and finally Stephanie's father lost hope. He abandoned the family, a broken man unable to cope. Stephanie heard he had become a street person. She neither knew nor seemed to care where he was.

Unable to afford housing in Toronto, Stephanie's mother had moved to the South Simcoe area of Oshawa, where rents were lower and from where she could commute to her job. But their financial situation remained desperate. There would be no Christmas tree, no Christmas feast and no Christmas gifts for Stephanie, as there had been in other years. There would be only sadness, and perhaps bewilderment that so many bad things could occur so quickly and with so little logic.

As Stephanie saw it, someone unseen and powerful, probably a man, had made a decision that cost her father his job. Her father, in turn, decided that his own family was either expendable or not worth fighting for, and he was gone. Now Doug, who in Stephanie's eyes was just another man with power, was practically haranguing her to be joyful, make decorations for her parents and get into the spirit of Christmas. Stephanie had no Christmas spirit; she simply had a reservoir of rage against people who had turned her world upside down, dumped her onto the cold ground and expected her to smile as though nothing had happened.

Stephanie's ordeal opened our eyes to similar problems facing other children in our school. We began to recognize and understand the unusual reaction of some students when facing Christmas, March break and summer vacation. Many children reacted by growing sullen, withdrawn and hostile. We discussed this with our counsellors, Debbie and Teresa. Debbie was a psychometrist and Teresa a social worker. Both explained that these children craved stability in their lives, and any break in school routine meant upheaval. Perhaps they would be shuttled between one parent's home and another like a piece of baggage, or they would lose a vital source of love and security when school was interrupted. Meanwhile, they were being encouraged to take part in what should be a joyous celebration, in total disregard of their inner pain. Was it any wonder that Stephanie finally exploded in anger and frustration?

We could not eliminate holidays and celebrations. We could, however, handle them differently to avoid raising expectations of things that might not occur. We dropped Christmas Decorating Days and avoided detailed classroom discussions of gifts at all festive occasions. None of this would solve the core problems of Stephanie and other children like her, but we hoped it would lessen the ache.

Many of the children at South Simcoe were more mature and worldly-wise than other kids their age in more affluent and prosperous areas of the city. They had been dealing for years with social agencies, charities and perhaps the police as well, and they knew both the power and the limitations of these organizations. They also accepted that their role in the family structure, as damaged as it might be, could include being victim, defender, negotiator and more. Yet, despite their problems at home, children remained loyal to their parents and suspicious of outsiders. Combine that with remarkable maturity and deep sensitivity, and you encounter someone like Melanie.

Slim, dark and obviously a budding beauty, Melanie was a twelve-year-old Grade Six student who carried herself with great poise, and was threatening to starve herself to death.

"That's what she has been telling the other kids," one of the teachers confided in me. "We know she's having problems at home, and she seems to have lost quite a bit of weight recently."

I agreed to have a chat with her.

Melanie entered my office as though walking into a theatre. She chose a chair, sat down, folded her arms and stared straight ahead, looking for all the world like someone waiting for the movie to begin.

My efforts to engage her in conversation produced nothing more than monosyllabic answers, until she finally tilted her head and smiled at me knowingly. "I know why you have me here, Mrs. Dean," she said. "Some people have told you that I'm not eating and you want to talk to me about it. Well, I don't want to talk about it. So you can stop beating around the bush. I'm used to dealing with people like you—"

I interrupted her there, asking what she meant by "people like you."

"Counsellors," she said. "People who try to get me to talk so they can help me." She straightened her back and lifted her chin. "I can help myself."

She was very impressive, and almost intimidating—or as intimidating as a twelve year old can be while sitting in a principal's office. "You're quite right," I said. "I want to help you because I care about you and I'm concerned about you. We are all concerned about you. Now, tell me why you are not eating anymore."

"It's my body, Mrs. Dean," she said with total politeness. "I'm entitled not to eat if I don't want to eat."

I felt I was no longer chatting with a child but debating with an adept adult. It may be her own body, I agreed, but I was her principal and it was my job to look after her. Again I asked her to explain why she was threatening to starve herself to death.

Still as polite as ever, she said it was none of my business.

It was time for me to become firm. "Look," I said. "You don't know me very well, and I don't know you very well. All you know about me is that I'm the principal in this school, and all I know about you is that you are not eating and you are threatening to harm yourself. I can't ignore that, because my job is to watch over the kids in my care. I'm worried about you, Melanie, and I want to help you. Why don't we at least get to know each other a little?"

This didn't work either. In fact she told me she wanted to leave the office.

"I can't let you go," I said, "without having some assurance from you."

Melanie threw me a knowing smile. "Sure," she said. "What do you want to hear?"

I told her I needed her to promise she would abandon her threat of starvation and resume eating. If she could not agree to that, she would leave me no choice but to call her mother. I might even have to call upon an agency for assistance.

This seemed to strike a nerve. "Why call my mother?" she said. "What about?"

I replied that her mother had a right to know about her condition.

"Sure, my mother would be worried," Melanie said. "But she has enough to worry about already, so don't call her." She was angry, but I could detect a pleading tone in her voice as well.

"Then why can't you help us solve this situation yourself?" I said, exploiting an opening. "If your mother is already having problems, why add more to her burden?"

It took some time, but Melanie began at last to discuss her feelings. She was not just trying to lose weight, she explained. She was not anorexic. But she was worried. What about? "Everything, just everything." School didn't interest her and life didn't interest her. Then she said in a chilling and serious voice, "I just want to die."

I had heard children say this before, but in fits of temper, anger or dramatic despair. Hearing this intelligent and composed girl say it as calmly as if she were asking to borrow a pencil was alarming. Thankfully, she knew the impact of the words as well, because she began quietly to sob. This was almost as painful as her words, but it also marked a breakthrough. Little by little, Melanie began to relax with me. I was careful not to say much; Melanie's words were more important than my own, although I told her several times that everyone at the school cared about her and was worried about her. "You don't have to handle this all by yourself," I assured her at one point.

"Sure," she said with a hint of sarcasm. "There are lots of do-gooders around who want to help. Do you know what their way of helping is? They'll take me away from my mother. They've done it before, and all it does is make me and my mother cry. We cry and cry, and the people think they're helping us."

Melanie's story was familiar—so familiar that it was almost predictable. Her mother was an alcoholic, living with an abusive man. Someone had advised Melanie to call the Children's Aid Society for help if things ever became intolerable at home, and so she had. The response of the CAS was to remove the girl from the home environment. "They took me away from my mother," Melanie recalled through flowing tears. "They left her alone with that guy and put me in a foster home with a bunch of crappy people who sat around and smoked and drank all day. *And I'm supposed to be helped by this?*"

I sympathized with the CAS staff, who I knew were understaffed and trying to do their best for the children.

"I'll tell you right now," Melanie went on. "If you call my mother or the CAS or anybody and tell them I said those things just now, I'll lie. I'll say I never told you those things, and you know what? My mother will back me up."

"But you also told me things were terrible at home," I reminded her.

"Sure they are!" she agreed. *"But why should I leave?* I want him to leave, but my mother is not strong enough to kick him out and . . . and she loves him."

She made a good point, identifying a serious flaw in the system . . . A weak woman invites an abusive man into her life, is unable to eject him for one reason or another, and society's answer is to remove the child from the situation, making the two innocent parties miserable. In response, Melanie had appointed herself her mother's protector.

When Melanie calmed down somewhat, she began negotiating like an adult. "I'll make you a promise that I'll eat tonight," she said, "if you promise not to call my mother."

I agreed, but not without some conditions. "The trouble is," I pointed out, somewhat appalled to discover myself bargaining with a twelve year old, "you'll know if I kept my promise, but I'll never know if you kept yours. I have to trust you to keep your word. If you say you'll eat dinner this evening, I'll count on you to be truthful."

Her reply was typically direct—and convincing, thank goodness. "I wouldn't say so if I wasn't going to do it," she said. "I don't need your approval."

Melanie was not, I realized, being disrespectful to me. She was simply determined not to be a victim.

I don't know for certain if she kept her promise to me that evening, but I know that she abandoned talk of starving herself to death. When we passed in the halls, I would smile and ask if she had eaten that day. Sometimes she would answer and sometimes she would simply smile warmly back at me, which was answer enough.

Melanie's attitude reminded us that welfare agencies alone are not the answer to the problems of our students. For one thing, their finances and staff always seem stretched to the limit. Just as problematic, however, is the "one size fits all" approach that many agencies are forced to take due to heavy caseloads. We need to find a method that acknowledges the unique needs and personalities of our children.

Finding effective answers to this enormous problem involves more from the participants than just the presence of parents, schools and social agencies. It needs a community-wide effort, and we were slowly demonstrating this fact at South Simcoe. For many years a kind of social regression had been occurring, and generation after generation had been entrapped in the poverty cycle.

Bobby, Melanie and the rest were not statistics. They were bright, innocent children who did not seek the situation they encountered day after day, and could not alter it except by employing drastic measures. You could not solve their problems by tossing a few pennies in their direction and mumbling a few promises. They needed a totally different approach, based on respect and love.

You could see it in their eyes.

There are many theories worth considering when dealing with social problems and their impact on children. But as Bobby and Melanie and many others proved, theory alone is simply not enough. It certainly wasn't enough for Barbara, a bright Grade Eight student who was moody and lethargic but, interestingly enough, always neatly dressed and well groomed.

Barbara often arrived late for school, without having completed her homework. Many days she didn't arrive at school at all. She seemed not to care about school, appeared to be steadily losing weight and denied the existence of any problems at home. This, of course, was not true. Barbara had many problems at home, and she simply refused to acknowledge them out of shame or out of fear that, like Melanie, she might be sent off to a foster home. Foster families may be safe and comfortable, but they aren't home to these kids. As hard as they work and as dedicated as foster parents might be, most kids prefer living with their biological parents.

It took time, but the total picture of Barbara's life eventually became clear to us in all its poignant detail.

Both of Barbara's parents had worked long hours in their struggle to raise six children, and when the parents separated Barbara was saddled with responsibilities at home. Washing her clothes, as well as the clothes of her younger brothers, was Barbara's job. Some days she was unable to complete her laundry work and was too ashamed to wear dirty clothes to school, so she simply stayed home. She also played more roles than being her brothers' laundress; in many ways she was their nanny, often dressing and feeding them, as well as a housekeeper, responsible for sweeping floors and performing other cleaning duties.

As if that weren't enough, Barbara's mother took in boarders, and the tenants often entered her room when Barbara was at school, stealing her belongings and invading her privacy. One of the boarders, a man in his twenties, frequently made lewd suggestions to her. With no lock on her door, she slept fitfully, afraid that he might enter her room at night.

Being frightened and overworked was just the beginning of Barbara's trials. Her chores at home left her no time to socialize with friends at school. She grew more isolated than ever, a condition made worse by her lingering pain over the breakup of her parents' marriage. She loved her father deeply, but saw him only two or three times a year, even though he remained in the city. Barbara's father favoured her older sister, a preference he never attempted to conceal. To top it off, Barbara's sister had achieved an excellent academic record, a feat Barbara was made aware of through repeated comments such as, "Why can't you be as smart as your sister?" or "Your sister would have no problem doing that!"

It does not take a degree in social work to recognize that Barbara's situation needed more than a standard-issue dose of welfare. Her already low sense of self-worth sank even lower, and she erected barriers to avoid suffering more pain from any source.

When the full measure of Barbara's situation became apparent, we all reached out to assist her. Often our efforts were rejected. "I don't want your help," Barbara would say. "I'm too stupid. Leave me alone. Don't try to help me. I hate all of you." At other times she might call us a bunch of "do-gooders" who only wanted to help her in order to make ourselves feel better. Then she might toss a book against the wall.

Once more: *You don't give up on kids*. You don't write them off just because their actions are annoying and hostile. You get to the root of the problem and help them find a solution.

We refused to give up on Barbara. We began by assuring her that she could take all the time she needed to talk about her problems with Teresa, our social worker. Some days her need wasn't an opportunity to talk. It was a chance to cry, all alone, for ten minutes in a closed, quiet room before emerging, ready to face the balance of the day. We grew determined that South Simcoe would be more than a school to her; it would be a safe refuge.

Things started to improve. Barbara became more trusting and perhaps more confident, although she suffered a setback when a boy began spreading false rumours about her. The boy even threatened to have his older sister, a high school student, physically assault her. While we helped her deal with that concern, we noticed Barbara was eating barely enough to keep herself alive, another symptom of self-worth problems.

Fortunately, we also began to recognize Barbara's exceptional problem-solving skills. She became an excellent source of help for younger students, and their response, along with our own words of thanks and encouragement, helped restore her self-respect and self-confidence. She needed that desperately. What she did not need were words of criticism about her lateness or poor attendance.

We had three years to address Barbara's dilemma before she moved on to high school. During that time we were able to make her feel stronger, which Barbara could use as the basis for her own growth, maturity and pride. She began to regain weight and to blossom, eventually being selected as the valedictorian for her graduation class.

Barbara's problems had seemed overwhelming to her, a mountain of difficulties that she felt incapable of overcoming. Had we simply criticized her for her late attendance and failure to complete her work assignments, we would have been adding to her burden and misery. Instead, we offered care, concern and love, and she used these as a foundation to build inner strength and resiliency . . . and to improve her life in ways she once believed were impossible to realize.

Chapter 8

The Right to be Respected

Every human being has the right to be respected and shares the responsibility to respect others. This was the guiding principle of our Respect program, and defined the way we conducted day-to-day interactions and dealt with each other, as well as what we stood for as a school.

All of us on staff became comfortable telling the children that we loved and cared for them, and that they could count on us to be there for them. We encouraged the children to talk with us openly about their feelings; we wanted them to understand that it was okay to feel frustrated, upset or angry, but it was not okay to hurt someone because of those feelings. They had to learn to redirect their feelings and their thoughts, and to look on the positive side. In this way, they would become strong enough to ignore situations that, in the past, might have ignited an angry response. These were practical applications of our basic Respect program.

Our Respect program was graphically depicted as a series of concentric circles (inspired by the lesson of my grandmother, of course) with Respect for Oneself at the centre.

Radiating from this were other circles, representing Respect for Others in the Classroom; Respect for Others in the School; Respect for the Family; Respect for the Local Community; Respect for the Environment; and Respect for Others in the Global Community—different cultures, races and backgrounds.

We taught lessons on how it looked, sounded and felt to be respected and respectful. We explained that respect for yourself influenced the way you dressed, the way you talked, the way you walked and carried yourself, and the things you put into your body.

The children loved the idea that respect worked both ways, and that we would be as respectful to them as we expected them to be towards us. They understood that the right to be respected brought with it the responsibility to respect others, and they quickly grasped all the implications of this approach.

Respect for others, for example, meant listening to someone else's point of view. It meant using care and compassion when dealing with the feelings of others, and putting yourself "in the other person's shoes" to fully understand their feelings.

Respect for others in the school meant responding with assistance when someone needed help, managing conflicts peacefully and solving problems respectfully, instead of resorting to bullying and fighting.

Respect for others in the local community meant treating neighbours in the way the children wished to be treated themselves—specifically targeting vandalism and shoplifting.

And respect for others in the global community meant accepting and appreciating the fact that everyone is unique and of worth, so teasing and taunting someone for their differences was simply not acceptable.

Remember Melanie, the anorexic, worldly-wise girl who rejected help from social agencies? She grew more and more confident as an individual, strong in her beliefs and in her expectations for herself and others. During her last year at South Simcoe, Melanie's physical development caught up with her mental maturity. To put it bluntly, Melanie was drop-dead gorgeous, a quality made even more striking by her new confidence.

One day early in Melanie's first year at high school, I received a telephone call from her new, and very agitated, principal. I knew this man well; most of our students attended his school after graduating from Grade Eight. He understood and supported our programs at South Simcoe, and was always courteous and amiable. This time he sounded perplexed at best.

"What the heck are you teaching your kids down there?" he said jokingly, but with a distinct edge to his voice.

It took me a moment to respond. "What do you mean?" I asked.

"I have one of your former students here in my office," he said, "who just told her teacher where to effing go. When the teacher sent her to my office, she called him every name in the book. I asked why she spoke like that to her teacher, and she said he wasn't being respectful to her. She said she's a human being and has the right to be respected by every-body. Where the heck did she get all that stuff?"

It was Melanie, of course. Fiery, mature, don't-mess-with-me, younger-than-she-appears Melanie. "We teach our students that they have the right to be respected," I assured him. "But we also teach them that they have to respect others as well. Obviously, she did not handle herself in a very respectful manner."

I asked to speak to Melanie, who came on the line sounding angry and depressed. I told Melanie that we missed her at South Simcoe, and in my brightest, most cheerful voice I asked how she was doing.

Melanie was having a bad day, which was hardly news after hearing the principal's comment. According to Melanie, she arrived in class that morning without completing her work. This wasn't the first time for Melanie, and the teacher responded angrily, refusing to accept her excuse. When he raised his voice, Melanie believed he was not showing her sufficient respect and raised her voice back at him. Unfortunately, she also added a few colourful and totally unnecessary words of her own. "I lost my temper," she agreed.

"How could you have handled this differently?" I asked.

"I know, I know," she mumbled. "But he wasn't respecting *me!*"

"You've backed your principal into a corner," I said. "You haven't given him many choices now. The bottom line is that you made a choice to swear at a teacher. I hope you understand there will be consequences to that. I'm asking you to accept them and learn from them. And please remember this: if someone is disrespectful to you and you stand up for yourself, it does not give you the right to disrespect them."

Melanie assured me she understood, and reluctantly agreed to apologize to both the teacher and the principal. She also promised to finish the assignment that had launched this whole incident, and to do another one suggesting ways to handle situations in which you do not feel you are receiving respect. This was the "making amends" portion of the school's response. She also promised to try very hard to be respectful to the teacher in the future. Melanie stopped by to visit me at South Simcoe a few days later, where we had a pleasant talk about high school, about how to deal with people who failed to respect us, and about life in general. She even spoke to the students about her own recent experience, and explained the importance of mutual respect to avoid such confrontations. When she finished, we hugged and wished each other good luck.

Unfortunately, Melanie needed more than luck. I discovered later that she dropped out of school in Grade Eleven, although she did return as a part-time student. You can't, as they say, win them all. You just try to save as many as possible.

We didn't win with Jared. We simply learned the limits of our ability to steer some kids from disaster.

A tall kid with an annoying swagger, Jared was transferred to us from Newfoundland and had attended twelve different schools by the time he landed at South Simcoe. He and I chatted together on several occasions, and whenever his attitude became too grating and aggressive, I found I could soften it with a gently scolding word or two.

Jared's constant relocation among schools had been disastrous for his education, among other things. Enrolled in Grade Seven late in the school year, he was unable to read at the Grade One level, even though he was almost fifteen years old. The die had been cast on much of his life. He began to hang out with older kids in the evenings and on weekends, many of whom had been charged with stealing cars and petty thievery. There were also rumours of drug dealing. Eventually, Jared ceased attending school completely, boasting to his friends that he was earning as much as a thousand dollars a week by selling narcotics. The police and the CAS became involved, but it was virtually impossible to enforce any ruling designed to return Jared to school, even with the co-operation of his father.

Within a few months of leaving South Simcoe, we heard rumours that Jared was working the streets of Toronto as a prostitute to support his drug habit. The news shocked us terribly. We had never had a student fall so far, so fast. Jared represented the limits of our ability to help the children. Even applying all we had learned by then, kids like Jared had suffered so deeply and for so long that our best efforts were not enough.

Jared demonstrated that self-respect and self-worth cannot be acquired overnight, even from a program that was proving so effective with many other children. To be most effective, they have to begin the process at a very young age.

Sometimes the rage inside children proved so intense that nothing seemed capable of relieving it.

Brenda was like that. Her moods ranged from sullen and morose to near out-of-control bedlam, and she had been in and out of various treatment programs over the years. At her most violent, Brenda would heave her desk and all its contents onto the floor before charging out of the classroom, and sometimes out of the school. Or instead of fleeing, she would lie down and scream at the top of her lungs, sharing her anger and agony with the entire school. At times like these she sounded like a wounded animal in pain, and when the screams finally subsided, she would curl into a fetal position and sob uncontrollably, like a lost baby.

Nothing in our training prepared us for this kind of behaviour. It was doubly frustrating because her moods were totally unpredictable. "Maybe it has something to do with a full moon," one of the teachers suggested, half seriously.

The moon had no effect on Brenda, but food did. On days when she arrived at school without breakfast, she was more prone to losing control. We realized this and offered her food, but Brenda rejected any direct effort to reach her. So we took an indirect approach: Jacki recruited Brenda to assist in distributing milk and healthy snacks to other children in the school. In this way she could help herself to food without feeling we had intruded into her life. Brenda felt good about helping others and ensuring they were well fed. Accepting responsibility also improved her sense of self-worth, and sometimes Jacki invited Brenda to the staff room to help wash dishes. Doing chores seemed to calm the girl, and gave her an opportunity to talk with someone who cared.

We made progress. But the steps were tiny.

Once, a student burst into my office to announce he had found Brenda lying in the middle of the busy roadway in front of the school, causing a major traffic tie-up. He tried to persuade her to get up, but she swore at him and refused to move, claiming no one really loved her or cared about her. Like Melanie, Stephanie and a few others, Brenda exhibited suicidal tendencies. In the midst of one of her outbursts she would scream, "I want to die!" and the agony in her voice would be almost too much to bear. "I don't know why they put me on this planet," she might wail. "I don't want to live anymore. I just want to die."

With help from Debbie and Teresa we learned how to handle Brenda's crises. She needed to hear that the feelings would pass and that things would get better. She depended on teachers to assure her of it, to the point where she began calling the staff at home during summer vacation, her voice sounding horribly alone, her words repeating her wish to die.

One evening she called Jacki at home, crying over the telephone. In the background Jacki could hear shouts of anger, and what sounded like someone thumping on a door or wall.

"What's that noise?" Jacki asked, and Brenda admitted she had locked her mother out of their apartment. Jacki suggested that she unlock the door and let her mother in.

Brenda finally agreed, but not until she explained her actions to Jacki. Her parents, Brenda complained, did not respect her. They also, it became clear, failed to live up to Brenda's rules of behaviour. As Brenda explained it, she had completed her housekeeping chores that morning in order to be permitted to attend a dance that night. But her mother broke her word and informed Brenda she could not attend the dance after all. To thirteen-year-old girls this simple incident can assume massive proportions of unfairness and disaster. To Brenda it represented yet more evidence of a corrupt world, one in which she no longer wanted to live.

Investigations by the police and CAS revealed extensive drug use in Brenda's home. Charges were laid, and Brenda was made a ward of the Children's Aid Society, placed in a foster home and transferred out of our area.

It was Brenda who had reported her own parents to the police.

Lack of a decent breakfast intensified Brenda's rage through the day, and this was not unusual among the children we encountered. Steve Ramsanker had taught me to recognize the connection between a full stomach and emotional stability, something he learned early in his career in Edmonton, where he introduced nutritious lunches and snacks as a key element of his school's program.

Those two needs—for food and affection—may appear unrelated, but they are primary nevertheless. Those of us who have never experienced intense hunger in the midst of plenty may have difficulty understanding such angry outbursts. Brenda's need for both food and affection had been unsatisfied. Others might have chosen a more passive reaction, but Brenda took a dramatic, aggressive posture.

So did thirteen-year-old Brad.

Brad arrived in mid-term during my first year at South Simcoe, and he provided one of my earliest lessons in handling very violent children. During his first week with us Brad was almost invisible, sitting quietly in class and taking part in few activities with other kids. This wasn't unusual for new students. Many were being moved constantly from place to place at the insistence of one parent or another, and it often took them some time to build close relationships among their peers.

One day Brad emerged from his shell. Or more correctly, a furious and violence-prone adolescent appeared. Brad's anger exploded, triggered by another student's word or gesture, and he threw a chair against a school window, cursed his teacher and everyone around him, and stormed out of the classroom and into the hall.

Alerted by his teacher, I went looking for Brad and encountered him in the hallway, walking back from the washroom towards class. His temper still raging, he was punching walls and kicking snow boots and other items down the hall ahead of him.

I said hello as he approached me.

"Leave me alone, you bitch!" he practically spat at me.

It was time to show authority. "I beg your pardon," I said

in my sternest principal's voice. "Do you know who I am? I'm the principal."

Brad was clearly unimpressed. "So what?" he snarled. "I don't care who you are. Just get out of my face, you stupid bitch!"

I was stunned. Over my years in education I had endured insolence and rudeness from students now and then, but never with this much hot anger fuelling the words. Brad was not going to respect me for my title alone, and short of suspension, no disciplinary action came to mind. I realized I had broken a cardinal rule by confronting an angry student, and made a decision to let him cool off first—something I should have done in the first place. So I turned on my heel and walked back to my office, leaving Brad standing there, looking for a fight.

Once in my office, I called a former colleague who had recently retired as a principal. I considered him a mentor and often asked his advice when handling situations such as this one. By this time Brad was standing outside my office door, not sure what to do and almost challenging anyone to approach him.

"It's nearly lunchtime," the former principal pointed out. "Why not get his lunch from his classroom, take it to your office, and let him know that when he wants lunch, he can get it from you there. Tell him he cannot go back into the classroom until the two of you have a talk."

It worked. On my way past Brad I casually mentioned that I had his lunch in my office, and that when the school bell rang at noon, he could come and get it. "Because you threw the chair," I said, "I cannot let you back into the classroom until we deal with that."

A few minutes after the lunch bell sounded, Brad

knocked cautiously on my office door and asked if he could have his lunch. I cheerfully pulled out a chair, handed him his lunch bag and invited him to sit down, as though nothing had happened.

"Let's eat our lunch together and chat," I said. My invitation surprised him; he had obviously been prepared for a tongue-lashing or at least some hint of immediate discipline. He sat down rather tentatively, and I watched, horrified, as he withdrew nothing from the paper bag but a canned soft drink and a package of soda crackers.

Does it make sense for a thirteen-year-old boy to become violent and aggressive as a result of hunger and malnutrition? Only a starving thirteen-year-old boy feeling a little lost and dislocated is qualified to answer that question with authority.

"You know," I said casually, unwrapping the sandwich I had brought for my own lunch, "I had something to eat earlier this morning and I won't be able to finish this sandwich. I hate to waste food. Can you help me out and take half for yourself?"

"Sure." Brad actually smiled at me. "I don't mind helping you out."

I had expected to review Brad's unacceptable behaviour while we ate our lunch. But the gratitude in his face, and the way he wolfed down my sandwich and the apple I offered him, made me change my tactics. Instead of discussing respect and our expectations of him, we talked quietly and struck a deal. The next time Brad felt himself growing angry, he could walk out of the classroom and use one of the school's designated safe places to cool off. "You have the right to be angry," I said. "But you don't have the right to use your anger to hurt or insult other people or throw furniture." I added that there would be consequences as a result of throwing the chair against the window and breaking it. Brad nodded his head in acceptance and agreement. Funny how a decent lunch can deactivate so much fury in a child. Or maybe it's not funny at all.

During the weeks following our encounter I made a point of seeking out Brad, to offer him a smile and a word of encouragement, and to ask if I could see his work. Brad needed two things. He needed a decent, regular diet; and he needed to know that we cared about him. Are hunger for food and hunger for affection really so different from each other? Maybe not.

There was no immediate, total transformation in Brad. Other incidents of anger and rage popped up from time to time, but they became less violent and occurred less frequently.

When I began to examine Brad's life in more detail, the source of his rage and frustration became obvious and understandable. He often went entire days without having much to eat, and the sight of other children eating their lunches must have driven him mad.

He wasn't alone. Some children caught shoplifting in stores at the mall across the street were stealing cookies, potato chips, soft drinks and candies because they were truly hungry. Was it wrong? Of course it was. Was it understandable? I leave it to you.

In response, we introduced our Healthy Snack program (now called Healthful Happenings), with help from nurses in our local Public Health department. It was run by one class and taught the children how to plan, shop for and prepare healthy snacks. In this program, groups of students visited classes, conducting a survey to determine who wanted snacks while at school. The surveying students were required to count the preferred snacks—cheese and apples, for example—and determine the quantity needed of each. For example, if seventeen children requested half an apple for their snack, the students conducting the survey had to translate this into the number of whole apples they would need, which gave the concept of fractions an entirely new meaning.

This tied neatly into their math studies, and improved their self-confidence, because the Grade Six kids had to approach students in Grades Seven and Eight for their opinions. Of course, the practical benefit to the staff was identifying the children who needed daily snacks in a manner that did not single them out.

At the start of the program, snacks were provided by staff members, who paid for the food out of their own pockets. I realized we couldn't continue to fund things in that manner, so we turned to our Kiwanis Club partners for help. They became involved, along with St. Vincent's Kitchen, and soon the children were munching on bagels, cheese and fruit, washed down with milk. If a child needed breakfast, it was provided for him or her as part of the school's everyday routine.

Why didn't the children receive decent meals at home? There were many reasons, most of them familiar and beyond resolution by the school alone. Many young mothers simply didn't know how to manage a household budget, or how to make inexpensive and nutritious meals. You could almost trace the income cycle of many families. At the beginning of each month, when funds were plentiful, the children arrived with full lunches. As the month progressed, the lunches grew leaner, until, during the last few days before the cheques arrived, they would often bring no food at all.

Some parents, whose incomes were strained by numerous expenses, were taking money from the food budget to buy clothing for their children. When it came down to providing either full breakfasts and lunches or a warm winter coat and hat, they chose the latter. This was something we could address with a clothing drive, so twice a year we "sold" clean used clothing collected from staff, family, friends, business partners and other sources. For ten cents or an item donated to the food bank, children and parents alike could choose whatever they needed, and every garment that left the school was, to us, a potential meal fed to the children in their homes. This was neither a sale nor charity; it was simply a method of distributing clothing to those who needed it, without offending their dignity.

We decided that we would celebrate our most respectful students, and let them know how much the entire community appreciated them and cared about them. The students themselves came up with the idea for a Respect Lunch, something we probably would not have thought of on our own.

The mood of the entire school began to change, but it is the effect of the Respect program on particular children that I remember most clearly—kids like twelve-year-old Roger, who arrived at South Simcoe late one spring from Toronto, bringing a long history of problem behaviour with him.

Roger had been disruptive in class during his tenure at other schools. He mimicked teachers and students, was frequently absent for days on end, and was considered a handful at the best of times—not the kind of student you want dropped into your classroom towards the end of the school year.

Regardless of his behaviour record, however, Roger quickly let us know how much he loved the school's Respect program, and how much he was looking forward to enjoying a Respect Lunch. By this time the Respect Lunch was attracting people from outside the school to act as servers, including senior officers from the Durham Regional Police Service.

"I'm going to get a lunch," he announced soon after arriving at school.

We reminded him that some students took an entire school year to qualify for a Respect Lunch, and Roger had arrived with barely two months remaining before summer vacation. Roger didn't care. He was determined to enjoy that lunch before the year was over.

His actions seemed to prove it. Every few days, knowing Roger's troubled history, I would check with his teacher to ask how he was doing. Each time, the response was more than encouraging—it was positively effusive, not to mention a major surprise to everyone who knew of Roger's school history. "I can't believe it," his teacher exclaimed at one point. "If all my kids were as well-behaved as Roger, my job would be such a breeze!"

The Respect program was working, we knew. But Roger's response was spectacular. Here was this really tough kids, who might have been expected to view the program rather cynically, changing his entire attitude and carriage. And he was a newcomer as well; our other students had had more time to understand and appreciate the Respect concept, but Roger grasped it immediately.

I called Roger into my office one day for a chat.

"I hear you cook a really good lunch," he said after settling himself in a chair.

"And I hear you've been an especially good student," I said. I told Roger I was very impressed with his work and behaviour. I also promised that I would personally cook his hamburger at the Respect Lunch. The lunch, I added, would be served by officers from the Durham Regional

Police, as well as our business and community partners plus parents and teachers.

His face lit up with anticipation. "It's a deal," he said, and practically bolted from my office, anxious, I'm sure, to boast about my offer to the other children.

Over the next couple of weeks Roger continued to be respectful, helping other kids and playing games with them. He was, quite simply, a model student, always wearing a pleasant smile and telling everyone how much he enjoyed "this respect thing," as he put it. Then, just two days before the Respect Lunch was scheduled, Roger's teacher stopped me in the hall. "Something's wrong with Roger," she told me, looking distressed. "He's not the same. He's acting strangely this morning."

I asked her to send Roger to my office, and the boy who entered looked very different from the one who had been determined to sit down to a Respect Lunch. This Roger hung his head, spoke in a low voice and carried himself as though he were about to flee, strike out or simply break down and cry.

"Roger," I said when he was seated, staring at the floor, "what's wrong?"

"My father was hurt last night," he said. "They took him to the hospital."

"What happened?" I ask. "Tell me about it."

I expected to hear about a traffic accident or an industrial mishap, perhaps a tumble off a ladder in his home. Instead, Roger blurted out, "He was hit with a machete, and they took him to the hospital. I don't know if he's OK or not."

I felt sick to my stomach. Suggesting I talk to his mother, I went to another telephone, called Roger's home, left my name and my reason for calling on the answering machine, and awaited a reply.

A woman who identified herself as Roger's mother called back a few minutes later. Instead of hearing the voice of a distressed parent, I found myself speaking with a woman who was annoyed with me and upset with her son. "Don't you people listen to the news?" she snapped. "Didn't you hear about a murder last night? I told Roger the guy was dead before he went to school this morning. Obviously, he wasn't listening."

I asked whom she meant by "the guy." Wasn't it Roger's father, her husband, who was killed?

"Naw," she said. "It was just a boarder who lived in the same house as us. He moved out a few weeks ago."

Only a year earlier I might have judged this woman for her harshness, and for her apparent insensitivity towards her son's feelings. But my experience with South Simcoe families had taught me a lesson about jumping to conclusions, so I kept talking with her, letting her lead the conversation. Gradually her voice became more emotional, and at one point, when I told her I understood her feelings, the line went quiet for several seconds. Then she began to cry. Whatever the relationship between her and the former boarder might have been, he apparently had been kind to Roger, taking the boy fishing and generally filling a father's role.

"If Roger doesn't know he's dead now," she said between sobs, "I can't tell him myself. Not right now. Not when I'm like this. Will you do it for me?" she pleaded.

I called Roger back into my office and told him I had been speaking to his mother about his "dad."

"Is he OK?" Roger said.

"People who get hurt as badly as he did," I said, "don't always turn out OK."

He pondered that for a moment. "Is he dead?" he asked.

"Yes," I said. "He is." I waited for the news to sink in. "Do you know what this means?" I said finally.

"Sure," Roger said. "He's gone to heaven."

To encourage him to release his emotions, I began talking as two saddened individuals, not as principal and student. "Roger," I said gently, "my father died recently and it was a terrible loss to me."

We talked for a while, long enough for Roger to describe the things he and his "dad" had done together.

"When my father died," I said, "I couldn't concentrate for a while. So you tell me: what do you want to do this morning? Go back to class? Maybe work on the computer for a while? Or just stay here?"

Roger said he would like to work on the computer until lunch, which sounded like a fine choice to me.

Roger went home for lunch and did not return to school for several days. Messages from me to his home, left on the answering machine, generated no response, and I feared we had lost him. We had grown close in a short time, Roger and I, and my heart ached at the pain and sadness I knew he was suffering. So I was surprised to see Roger appear on the day of our Respect Lunch. He remained subdued, but talked easily with me when I told him how pleased we were to see him. "You worked hard for this meal," I said at one point.

"It wasn't just for the food," he admitted. "I wanted to eat lunch with everybody, and I wanted to see if the policemen would really serve me."

Watching him during the meal, I realized how important it was for Roger to feel part of our special group. He felt he belonged with the teachers preparing the meal (yes, I cooked Roger's hamburger, exactly as he ordered it), and with the smiling police officers and partners serving it to the children. He wanted to be part of that warmth and togetherness.

We never saw Roger again. Sometime during the following summer he and his mother moved out of the South Simcoe area, as so many children did. I knew we had made a difference in Roger's life, if only for a short time. Whatever trials he faced through the rest of his childhood, I hoped he would carry the warm memory of that special Respect Lunch with him, and remember what it felt like to be respectful and respected.

Was it wise to recognize children for respecting themselves, others around them, the community and the environment? I have never doubted the wisdom of the idea. We needed to break a cycle of behaviour among South Simcoe kids. It's difficult to retain your self-respect, or your respect for others, when you are the innocent target of abuse, denial and neglect. We needed to demonstrate to the children that they could change their behaviour and feel good about doing it. We needed to model the actions we wanted to see, and provide the students with the opportunity to practice being respectful.

During one of our Respect Lunches, Staff Sergeant Bill Temple of the local police force talked to the students as they ate their lunch. Towering over the children in his service uniform and flashing a warm smile, he told them, "You must always try to respect yourself and other people because it's a good thing to do," he said. "Most times in life, no one will even notice what you do. You keep doing it because it's the right thing, and doing the right thing makes you feel good. That's what life is all about—feeling good about yourself, being strong inside, and helping others to feel the same way."

I couldn't have said it better.

Chapter 9

· · · · · ·

Programs and Progress

Our Respect program and the Respect Lunches were working. Smiles were everywhere, daily goals were being achieved, and the energy level was wonderful to behold.

But the most significant change was in the actual process of teaching and learning. Instead of classroom rules, we developed classroom *agreements*—standards of behaviour and expectations, jointly established by both teachers and students. By using agreements instead of rules, the children began taking greater responsibility for their own behaviour. The teachers, relieved of much of the energy and attention usually dedicated to enforcing rules, discovered they enjoyed time to share in the joy of the children when goals were achieved, and take pride in watching an entire class progress in abilities and confidence.

Some problems remained, however, both in the classroom and in the schoolyard. We were still experiencing incidents of bullying and fighting, and the more we improved the atmosphere inside the school, the more concerned we became about the situation on the school playground. The problem was not exclusive to South Simcoe, of course; similar incidents were happening elsewhere, growing almost as prevalent among girls as among boys.

Several studies suggest schoolyard bullying is not only more prevalent than in the past, but is also growing more vicious and dangerous. A generation ago, schoolyard fights were conducted with fists; today they can involve knives and other weapons. Similarly, schoolyard bullies are no longer rogue kids, strutting around a playground to demonstrate their physical supremacy, like male lions defining their territory. Violence in schools can include entire gangs of children who may swarm their victims, goading each other on to more and more vicious actions. None of this, by the way, is confined to at-risk communities; the sad truth is, these incidents can occur anywhere in the world.

What's causing all this terrible violence? Several factors have been identified, but two seemed to keep recurring.

Both the bullies, and the children they choose as their targets, exhibit low levels of self-worth—a factor I found highly enlightening. Raise the self-worth of children generally, and you reduce not only the number of bullies but also the number of kids they target for their aggression. Kids who feel good about themselves, and strong inside, neither harass others nor accept abuse.

This solution defies the approach advocated by many who believe stricter discipline is the answer. We didn't believe the solution lay in "giving them a taste of their own medicine"; we were insistent, however, on bullies accepting meaningful consequences to their actions, making amends to their victims, and assuming ownership of the problem they created. Instead of punishment, our focus was getting to the root of the problem and preventing a recurrence.

Reducing schoolyard violence by raising self-worth is not muddle-headed theory. It works in practice, as we proved time and again at South Simcoe with children like Fred.

Fred was a Grade Eight student who took pleasure in taunting and teasing other children for his own amusement. He especially delighted in making offensive remarks to girls, ridiculing them until they burst into tears, then pretending he had done nothing wrong.

Fred's basic problem was his lack of connection; he was convinced nobody cared about him, and his actions seemed dedicated to proving this true. Each Monday, after spending the weekend with his mother, Fred appeared at school with a clean shirt, well-pressed trousers and freshly washed socks. From Monday to Friday, while he lived with his father, his clothing often reeked of cat urine, his hair was unclean and uncombed, and his socks would become so filthy that the fabric on the soles would harden like cardboard. In the class-room, children avoided sitting next to Fred because of the foul odor that floated around him like a cloud.

Kim, Fred's teacher, and Susan, Kim's teaching assistant, addressed the situation by introducing a special session in hygiene during regular Health class. No one needed it more than Fred, of course, and this was a convenient way to address Fred's problem without singling him out from the rest of the children. During hygiene classes, the teachers showed the children how to scrub their feet and trim their toenails with clippers. During an early hygiene class Kim shampooed Fred's hair and Susan, a former hairdresser, cut and styled it for him. When they finished, the other children actually compli-mented Fred on his appearance, oohing and aahing over him. Some actually told him he was handsome.

This admittedly had nothing to do with the traditional "three R's," but it made the children feel good about themselves, and the impact of that single achievement was far-reaching. The first time Fred saw himself with clean, well-groomed hair, he blurted, "I look so good, I feel like a king!"

Another factor in the rising incidence of schoolyard bullying and fighting may be the excessive unsupervised time children spend watching violent television programs. While this does not necessarily trigger direct acts of aggression, or spontaneously turn a good kid into a bully, some programs can make violence appear more acceptable by desensitizing the children.

To tackle the problem at South Simcoe, I read the work of many people who addressed this problem through research and studies. Most agreed that, in extreme cases, children need clinical counselling to change their behaviour, a solution far beyond the means of public schools. But attitudes can be modified among the majority of students who support fighting and bullying either actively, by following a gang leader, or passively, by providing an audience for bullies while they attack their victims.

The presence of an audience is a major incentive to bullying behaviour. When students watching the attack remain silent, they support the bully's actions by convincing him—or, increasingly, her—that they, the audience, are being intimidated. The bully uses this awareness to counter his or her low self-worth. Bullies may feel they are nobodies; if their peers fear them, the bullies grow convinced that they are now *some*bodies. Whether through silent assent or active support, bullies seem to need an audience to witness their behaviour. Without one, their aggression loses much of its lustre.

The good news? We found that extending our Respect program to address the schoolyard bullying and fighting problem, supported by visits from police officers to the school to discuss the subject, reduced the problem significantly. The officers chatted to the children in a non-threatening manner, talking about the dangers of gangs and the reasons behind bullying and fighting. They engaged in role playing, demonstrating how bullies can be discouraged from their behaviour, and how to avoid becoming a bully's victim. Many children simply needed to understand the seriousness of bullying and fighting. Violence should be regarded not as an inevitable experience in childhood, but as unacceptable behaviour that needs to be understood and addressed. Teresa and Debbie assisted us in developing and refining strategies to deal with bullying.

The link was clear: As children develop a deep sense of respect for themselves and others, bullying and fighting decrease. They recognize the importance of standing up to bullies as a group or, at the very least, turning their back on unacceptable behaviour and denying the bully the audience that he or she craves. This takes both courage and character, but time and again it proves effective.

To help children deal with bullying, we instituted school-yard agreements. Everyone decided it was necessary to banish bullying, fighting, teasing and taunting, and any-one involved in that kind of behaviour, by definition, broke the agreement.

A new student caught breaking the agreement, for example, would receive a warning. If it happened again, I would call the student to my office for a serious discussion about the agreement, and explain that such behaviour was unacceptable. "That is not the way to respect others," I would say, "or to respect yourself." When necessary we suspended the student and probed aspects in his or her life that might be causing the behaviour. Then the teachers and I would begin building a relationship with the child.

I was especially concerned about bullies and schoolyard fights because, as principal, teachers expected me to lay down the law with the kids. That was fine with me, except that I found so much of my time being devoted to this single problem that I couldn't find sufficient time for dealing with curriculum matters.

While we were teaching that bullying and fighting were unacceptable, we were also teaching the concept of working together to achieve common goals and *peer interdependence*. This became a major challenge, especially with students such as Tom when he and two other Grade Eight boys began bullying younger students. Tom and his buddies wanted to create a neighbourhood gang because, they believed, gangs earned "respect." They were basically good kids who discovered how to flex their muscles and intimidate others, even while participating in school programs designed to counter these same activities.

I learned about Tom and his gang activities shortly before one of our Respect Lunches. Tom's other actions entitled him to be part of our upcoming Respect Lunch, which created a dilemma. If he joined the group at the Respect Lunch, it would appear that we were overlooking his behaviour as a bully. If we excluded him, we would be breaking an agreement. Our kids, I knew, had experienced too many broken promises in their young lives; they didn't need another one from us.

So we compromised. Tom would be served his meal as promised, but not in the staff room with the other children. He would eat it in my office, with me present. And that's what we did. I served him with a smile at a table in my office. While Tom ate, I explained that he deserved his lunch, but that his bullying behaviour did not qualify him to enjoy the company of the other students. He finished his lunch in silence while I sat at my desk and read some reports. Then I asked if he had enjoyed it.

"Not really," he frowned. "It would have been a lot nicer if I had been in the staff room with the other kids. It was no fun eating by myself."

As much as anyone in the school, Tom wanted acceptance, recognition and the family atmosphere created during our Respect Lunches, with the participation of teachers, parents and our community partners. Tom was disappointed, but he understood the reason behind our decision and agreed that it was fair. More important, he learned a lesson about respect and confirmed it when he became a model student who often went out of his way to help others both in and out of school.

Bullying and violence at South Simcoe were not restricted to boys. One of the most aggressive and angry students I encountered was Meredith, a bright Grade Seven girl with an angelic face and cold, hardened eyes. I don't recall encountering a child with both more promise and more rage than Meredith. She refused to be touched, either physically or emotionally. Just eleven years old, Meredith was already associating with much older children in the evenings and on weekends. Many of her friends already had arrest records for car theft and other crimes.

Over time, I watched in horror as Meredith's actions grew

ever more intense. Her penchant for violence was shocking. On one occasion Meredith fought with a girl so furiously that she broke the other girl's nose. Many of her physical attacks appeared totally spontaneous, without cause or provocation. Consequences meant nothing to Meredith. If she grew bored or angry in class, she would simply rise from her seat, walk out of the school and go home. When taken to court by the attendance counsellor, and warned by a judge, Meredith simply turned on her heel and left the court-room in the middle of the warnings and admonishments.

Much of Meredith's life had been spent with various foster families, and she was receiving counselling from social agencies. While Meredith attended South Simcoe, she resided with a woman in her thirties whom we assumed was her mother. She wasn't. The woman was Meredith's grandmother.

Although we quickly formed some suspicions about the source of Meredith's rage, there was much in her life that we did not know for certain, and Meredith herself made it clear that she would not discuss the matter. Yet we grew deter-mined to help Meredith if we could. It was impossible not to feel sorry for someone so young, with so much anger boiling within her.

The attack in which Meredith broke her opponent's nose was a clear signal that the counselling efforts were not working. We could no longer risk injuries to other children. Home instruction was one possible approach, but social agencies familiar with Meredith's situation sug-gested it would be too dangerous to send a teacher to her home. What's more, Meredith's instantly negative reaction to the idea of staff entering her home made it even less prac-tical. Looking for some guidance, I raised our predicament with officials at the board office, who suggested we use a library.

Give me a break, I said to myself. Where was I to find a local library?

A little later I happened to be chatting about the problem with Louis, the manager of the Kmart store directly across the street. I expected to receive nothing more from him than a nod of sympathy. Instead, Louis asked how often I would need space for Meredith's special instruction periods.

"About one hour, three days a week," I said.

"Why not use my office?" he suggested.

I was stunned, and deeply touched. Here was the manager of a major department store, who faced dozens of crises each day—including, unfortunately, the odd incident involving a South Simcoe student—and still he was willing to relinquish his office space three times a week. But Louis wanted to help, and he believed both Meredith and South Simcoe were worth it. His suggestion demonstrated the depth of support we had managed to garner from our community partners, and Kim began escorting Meredith to the office for the special instruction Meredith needed.

Meredith's situation? You probably already guessed it. She was the victim of incest, a bright and attractive child who tried to balance her desire for a true childhood with her inner shame and disgust the only way she knew how—by lashing out at the world around her, especially anyone who threatened more pain and humiliation. My heart broke for her, and once again I was reminded of the practical limitations imposed on me and the school system generally. We simply could not solve all the problems we faced.

Meredith responded well to instruction from Kim. But just as we began feeling good about this small measure of progress, Meredith became pregnant, even before she experienced her first menstrual period, and she was removed from her environment by the Children's Aid Society. I wish we had had an opportunity to work with Meredith earlier; I am convinced we could have helped her avoid so much tragedy and pain.

Inspiring self-worth in children and teaching them how to control and deal with their anger, represented two basic goals in our program. We agreed to deal with the situation as a team, and over time we established some guidelines for the staff to follow when beginning the process of dealing with bullies and schoolyard fights:

- *Be available.* Help the children to resolve their conflict.
- *Listen to what each child has to say.* Let each tell his or her story; let him or her "get it off his/her chest."
- *Judge not.* Avoid assigning blame. Remember that there is a lot more to the story than you may be hearing.
- *Understand.* Appreciate the emotional level each child is attempting to deal with—anger, frustration, pain, etc.
- *Give love and support.* Empathize, do not sympathize.
- *Help them make a choice.* Assist the children to choose between withdrawing quietly to a safe place to calm down, or taking part in some calming activity.

Along with personal self-worth, I wanted South Simcoe to generate collective pride and build identity. We had a motto (*Together We Light the Way*), but I wanted something more to express what we stood for—something that the children could participate in, to express their pride and identity. A school song would do the trick. Sharon McLean, a supply teacher and I set to work writing the words and choosing a melody. The song summed up, I believe, so much of the atmosphere we were trying to create, and the goals we had set for ourselves and the children:

> *We are the children who are looking to the future,*
> *Sharing pride and singing our school song.*
> *At South Simcoe School, we're learning every day*
> *If Together We Light the Way, we will be strong.*
>
> *We learn the skills that are going to shape our lives,*
> *The sense of self that a good beginning gives.*
> *And every day we're sharing with our teachers and our friends*
> *Who will help us all become the best we can.*
>
> *We are the children who are looking to the future,*
> *Sharing pride and singing our school song.*
> *At South Simcoe School, we're learning every day*
> *If Together We Light the Way, we will be strong.*
> *If Together We Light the Way, we will be strong.*
> *So Together Let's Light the Way, and we'll be strong!*

We taught our school song to the students, and each class began singing it every morning, immediately following the national anthem. I would walk from class to class, listening to the children in each room, and stop to congratulate those who sang lustily and well. Only the Grade Eight kids tended to disappoint me, but that was understandable: by age thirteen or fourteen certain kinds of public display can be awkward for many children. I knew the younger students considered Grade Eights as models, and I didn't want the reticence of the seniors filtering down through the grades.

I wanted the children to demonstrate pride in their school, which by extension would be a method of showing pride in themselves. The more we demonstrated our pride as a group, the more pride we would have in ourselves as individuals. Singing was a fine way of expressing that feeling.

So was our school chant:

> *At South Simcoe*
> *We all know*
> *We're the best*
> *Yes! Yes! Yes!*

> *At South Simcoe*
> *We will, we will*
> *Rock you!*

Each time I recall our school song, I think of Meagan, and a host of emotions washes over me.

We were holding regular school assemblies at the Legion Hall, and these were a confirmation of success to us. The behaviour of the children during our assemblies was wonderful to see. We used these events to reinforce all the principles we stood for—and the children learned to respect them—as well as to honour the involvement of all who participated.

We ended each assembly by having the entire school sing the school song with joy and vigour. When we first began, the senior students had difficulty overcoming their adolescent self-consciousness about singing in the midst of assemblies. Perhaps, I thought, the kids will sing louder if some of their peers were leading them at the microphone, so I asked for volunteers to lead the school in singing our song. Among the small number who offered to perform the task was Meagan.

I was taken aback. Meagan was a thin waif of a girl with huge, heart-breaking eyes ringed in dark circles, and the sad look of a fetal alcohol child. Sweet and good-natured, Meagan had never shown any such initiative in the past, and standing at a microphone in front of two hundred classmates, leading them in singing, is not customarily an ambition for shy and introverted children. But Meagan seemed determined, and how could I refuse her?

After I introduced the song leaders at the next assembly, Meagan seized the microphone in her tiny hand, positioned herself in the centre of the group, and burst into song with a powerful bell-like voice, exhorting the other students to raise their voices with her. She sang with such power and confidence that we asked her to repeat the performance at subsequent assemblies. During one of them, a Toronto TV station arrived to tape a three-part series on the school and captured Meagan's exuberant performance.

Meagan's family background was in sharp contrast to her marvellous onstage persona. On the occasions when Meagan and I chatted, she spoke sadly of her treatment at home, and complained of her parents' excessive drug use. Like so many children I encountered at South Simcoe, Meagan was forced to deal with a wide gulf separating her life at school from her life at home. School was a place where she could count on being loved and cared for, a place where she received recognition and admiration for her talent. At home, little attention was paid to her needs as a young girl; no one seemed interested in her accomplishments, and the pain must have been very real and very deep to her.

Meagan was not dealing with her situation alone, and that both encouraged and frightened her. The Children's Aid Society had been aware of her home life, and caseworkers were monitoring Meagan's treatment, supported by information we provided on request. Knowing someone was watching and caring for her may have been encouraging to Meagan, but she also knew there was a possibility of being removed from her home environment, and this alarmed her.

Finally, a decision was made to relocate Meaghan, and when the CAS worker arrived at the school to carry out the order, we called Meagan to join us. At the news that she would be sent to a foster family, Meagan rushed across the room and into my arms, crying uncontrollably. "You guys care about me!" she sobbed, begging Jacki or me to take her. "Why can't I stay with you? Why am I being sent away to some strange family?"

Jacki and I were on the verge of tears as we sat with Meagan while the CAS worker explained where she was going and why. Thankfully, the Society arranged for Meagan to continue attending South Simcoe, where she could count on being loved and appreciated. In this manner, only one aspect of Meagan's life was being changed. Still, wrenching a child from her parents, no matter how necessary a move it may seem, is always agonizing to watch.

Once the pain of separation began to fade, the transformation in Meagan was gratifying. She arrived at school with clean, well-brushed hair and wearing attractive clothes, and she walked with more confidence than I had seen in her. Meagan missed her parents terribly, and she agonized over reporting their drug use, even though she knew she had done the correct thing. She continued to lead the school in singing, but with a hint of sadness and regret in her large eyes, one that I suspected would remain there for a long time.

We wanted the students to return home at the end of each school day knowing they had achieved something vital in their lives and looking forward to returning the following day. So every morning in every classroom (yes, even kindergarten), students set daily goals for themselves. At the end of the day they reflected on their activities, decided if their goals had been accomplished and selected a focus for the next day. By emphasizing a daily sense of accomplishment over and over, the children began building a sense of self-worth and self-confidence.

As the year unfolded, we realized how important the act of reflection was in our strategy to raise the self-worth of our students. Reflection helped them identify and enjoy the positive things in their lives. Even when they were not able to accomplish a major goal for that day, the children were asked to identify something else they had achieved. Every day, we assured them, something positive can happen. They could not allow one bad thing to crowd many good things out of their minds and leave them feeling depressed or frustrated.

The children gradually needed less and less teacher involvement in their goal-setting and reflection. Developing a sense of control and a remarkable resilience, they learned to think for themselves and create a strategy to achieve their objectives. They built on a series of small successes, each adding to the overall weight and impact of the others, to produce three major results:

1. They learned to take responsibility for their actions and experience pride in their achievements.

2. They discovered they had control over their lives during the school day.

3. When they left school at the end of each day, they felt good about themselves, raising their overall sense of self-worth.

Many of the children still needed many things in their lives, and some were beyond the scope of our abilities to provide. Fortunately, self-worth and respect were two of their most critical needs, and we were able to furnish both in the hearts and minds of the students. Their impact, and the core of confidence they provided, made all of our other achievements possible.

Chapter 10

· · · · · · ·

The Circle of Love

Something unique was happening at our school, a change so profound and positive that one of our community partners called it a revolution of the heart.

As the skeptics grew silent, others grew intrigued and supportive. We relished and embraced assistance from many sources, and in at least one instance the help proved literally life-saving.

One of the organizations that offered to assist us was St. John's Ambulance. Our friend George, one of our most enthusiastic partners, happened to mention that the Kiwanis Club funded a booklet used in a course on babysitting conducted by St. John's Ambulance. The course was being taught to neighbourhood teenagers on Saturdays.

It occurred to me that many of the children in our school could benefit from this training. I knew first-hand that children ten years old or even younger were being assigned to care for younger brothers and sisters. We couldn't change the circumstances that led parents to place so much responsibility on the shoulders of such young children; but we could help our students cope with the situation. We could also improve their confidence and sense of self-worth, two keystones in our efforts to help the kids grow more resilient. And if we could provide them with a job skill, wouldn't that be worth pursuing?

If St. John's Ambulance could teach a babysitting course in the neighbourhood on Saturdays, perhaps they could teach one to the students in school during the week. This would mean reassigning some time out of the school day for participants in the course—a decision to be taken only if the parents agreed that it made sense. My assessment of new ideas remained, *What's in the best interests of the kids?* In this case some basic training in babysitting would benefit everyone, and when the majority of parents said, "Let's do it!" we did.

Among the students who completed the course was Susan, an attractive fourteen year old frequently called upon by her mother to babysit Susan's four-year-old sister and seven-year-old brother. One evening Susan and another Grade Eight student were babysitting the children when the seven year old refused to obey a request from his older sister. Susan, in an attempt to persuade him to see things her way, threatened to complain to their mother, noting that the mother would likely remove the boy's bike-riding privileges. In anger, the boy pulled a large kitchen knife from a drawer and hurled it in Susan's direction, missing her but striking his four-year-old sister in the leg.

The blade nicked an artery. Blood splattered everywhere, and as the little girl shrieked in pain and horror, the training Susan and her friend had received from St. John's Ambulance kicked in. They staunched the flow, called 911, and rushed the child outside to meet the ambulance as it arrived.

At the hospital, surgeons noted that the little girl might easily have died from loss of blood had Susan and her friend not acted so quickly. The CAS persuaded Susan's mother to leave her job and accept mother's allowance, enabling her to care for her children herself, and her son was enrolled in a special counselling program. Susan, of course, had proven the value and wisdom of the babysitting course in a true life-or-death situation. It also validated my decision to take time from school activities for the course. Education, I realized, could not end at the playground gate. Nor could the demands of life stop there. They both worked best when integrated—when social issues reached into the school, and when education extended into the needs of home and family.

The number of our community partners continued to grow, and their value to the children continued to increase. Various branches of Kiwanis, St. John's Ambulance, several mall merchants, the local police force and the Canadian Legion had formed the early core of supporters, and other organizations were being added month by month. Within just a few years South Simcoe Public School had become a symbol of change and improvement.

Other programs were introduced and added to the Respect program, creating a multifaceted structure encompassing all the goals and objectives we had set. "It's a little like cooking three or four meals on the same stove," I explained to someone. "They're all bubbling away, and every now and then you have to pay first this one, then that one, some attention. You stir it, you sample it, you season it, then you move on to another." That's what it was like managing the various programs at South Simcoe.

Our Triple-S program, for example, complemented our Respect program and supported its guiding principle.

Triple-S helped achieve the goal of building respect for one-self and for others by asking students to act in an intentional and deliberate manner. We encouraged students to become active in Scholastics, Sports and school activities, and Service to the school and the community. The service category was a critical part in our effort to teach the concepts of taking responsibility for one's community and being a good citizen, and it honoured students who had demonstrated service.

My approach had its roots in yet another lesson learned at my grandmother's knee. She taught me that we all have something to give, and that even if we have nothing to share in terms of material things, our time and love are the greatest gifts we can offer.

She told us that a wise man in India had said, "The greatest gift you can give is your time and your love." Years later I discovered that the man she referred to was actually Rabindranath Tagore, who won the 1913 Nobel Prize for Literature, and his actual words were: "The greatest happiness in life is in service to mankind." I have learned that children are quick to grasp the idea of giving their time. They love to play a role in the community, and they especially enjoy the good feelings they get from providing service to others.

Teachers and children alike worked together to determine different ways of giving back to the community. Someone pointed out that seniors in the area had difficulty walking to the store for a newspaper or other items. They lacked the mobility and energy of youth, which the children possessed in abundance, so this was quickly identified as one kind of service to be provided. Another service might be shovelling snow from the sidewalk for someone who lacked the ability to do it herself. A dozen other ideas were proposed: visit someone in the hospital or at a nursing home, take non-perishable items to the food bank, join a partner in the annual Terry Fox Run to raise money for cancer research, or simply walk through the neighbourhood picking up garbage.

These activities were tracked and, at the end of each term when report cards were issued, each student who performed an appropriate service was honoured with an "S." An "S" from each of the three categories provided the student with Triple-S recognition. The idea struck a responsive chord with the children for a reason that, frankly, had never occurred to us. "You know what I like about Triple-S?" a student said to me one day. "It's just for us. Report cards, they're for our parents, but when all these important people come to see us, it makes us feel really good. It shows they care about us."

The staff ensured that all students had the opportunity to be honoured and recognized during the Triple-S assemblies. With a little effort, every child could qualify for an "S," and they all did. All, that is, except Fred.

Fred had been gaining confidence and pride in himself as a result of the attention we paid to grooming. But he remained a Grade Eight student functioning at a Grade One level, filled with enough anger and frustration to prevent him from participating in Triple-S. From time to time Fred still insulted his teacher or threw a tantrum serious enough to send him to my office, where he would eventually mumble an apology and offer to make amends. During one of these sessions I commented that Fred had not made an effort to obtain a single "S."

"And I won't," Fred almost sneered. "I'm not doing nothin' to help nobody."

Fred seemed determined, which was unfortunate in my view. By refusing to participate, he was alienating himself still further from the rest of the children.

One day when Fred was walking down the hall towards a classroom, he passed a windowed door with a large smudge or smear on the glass. As I stood watching, open-mouthed, he stopped, unconsciously withdrew a tissue from his pocket and began wiping away the spot.

I couldn't contain my excitement. "Fred!" I shouted. "You're doing something for the school! You're performing a service! That's terrific!"

Fred froze on the spot, unsure what would happen next.

I called Fred's teacher, Alvena, out of her classroom, and Kim Hutchinson came running down the hall from the other direction at the sound of my voice. "Look," I said to them, pointing at Fred. "He's cleaning the window in the door. He's performing an act of service for the school."

Fred grinned a little and resumed polishing the glass. Kim ran to her room and returned with a cleaning rag. "Here," she said, handing it to Fred, "this will work better than that old Kleenex," and Fred took it from her and kept polishing.

"You know," I said to Kim and Alvena as we stood back and watched him work, "Fred has definitely made a choice to do something for the school. What do you think?" They agreed he had.

All right, it was pushing things a little, I suppose, but Fred was obviously proud that he could now be included in the Triple-S program, whether he had intended to perform a service or not. What's more, he polished that particular pane of glass virtually every day for the rest of his time at South Simcoe.

Our first Triple-S ceremony was held in March 1993, and no Academy Awards ceremony was orchestrated with more attention to detail and emotional impact. We built in enough pomp and circumstance for a Buckingham Palace reception, and the kids loved it. The formality, music, staging and speeches all made them walk a little taller and prouder, and to this day, Triple-S ceremonies throughout the Durham District maintain the same theme, elements and atmosphere.

As the children entered the Legion Hall in a procession for that first presentation, the theme music from *Chariots of Fire* played through the speakers of the sound system. Before the actual ceremony began, two senior students mounted the stage to slowly unfurl a banner displaying our motto *Together We Light the Way* and our logo. The audience sat in hushed silence, and the children's faces shone with pride. Several invited guests, including our community partners and school custodians, were on hand to share in the celebration. I remember Sharon McLean reaching to squeeze my hand. "This is it, Sandra," she said. "We're really beginning to make a difference now." We both had tears in our eyes.

Meanwhile, the children were growing more and more enthralled with the ceremony. The names of the first few children to be honoured, and the Triple-S activities in which they had been involved, were read solemnly over the sound system, and the audience applauded with enthusiasm as each student stepped up to the podium to receive his or her certificate.

The attention paid by the other students, the staff and the invited guests was obviously important to the children. So were the descriptions of the actions behind the Triple-S recognition. We took the time to describe each in detail— "Joey helped at Parent Rap sessions by babysitting. He also performed acts of service in the community by shoveling snow from his neighbour's walk"—providing the students with positive behavioural models from their peers.

Why all the solemn formality? We had several reasons. We wanted everyone to recognize the importance of the Triple-S program to our overall approach in educating the children—especially building a foundation of self-worth among the students. We also wanted to honour both the achievements of the children, and the presence of so many guests and community partners at the event. But most of all we wanted the children to remember the ceremony in detail, and to understand that the joy of that day would remain in their hearts forever.

At the end of the first Triple-S ceremony we revealed our pièce de résistance. Kim Hutchinson, who was a great bargain hunter, had spent several days searching local costume houses for a shark outfit. It was not easy; a shark costume is not a common party outfit in our part of the world. She finally managed to find a costume so worn and moth-eaten that the rental company sold it for just a few dollars. With a little sewing, stitching and patching by her mother-in-law, Pauline, it was made as good as new. As our Triple-S ceremony was ending, we announced the arrival of a special guest: South Simcoe Public School's own mascot, Sharkie. Kim appeared dressed in the costume as wild cheers exploded from the students.

Everyone wanted to hug our mascot "Sharkie," and almost every student did. At that point we knew without any doubt at all that our dream of building pride and achieving wonders at South Simcoe Public School was beginning to come true. These children, many of whom did not enjoy the opportunities available to students in other schools in the area, had grown proud of their school, proud of their achievements and, most importantly, proud of themselves.

When it came to community involvement, the activity that seemed to produce the most enthusiastic response was our Circle of Love: Reading Together program. The simple act of reading to children yields many wonderful benefits. It builds a love of books and reading for the kids, it makes the grown-ups feel good, and it generates a bond between adults and children. Each time our community partners read to the children, it made the kids feel they were important and made the adults feel needed. The chemistry generated by this special bonding is difficult to describe. Perhaps Rob Pitfield, our partner from ScotiaBank, put it best when he said, "It's like magic!"

Interestingly enough, many of the community partners who agreed to read to our children soon resumed reading to their own kids at home. One partner confessed that he thought reading stories aloud to his children ended when they learned to read for themselves. He changed his mind, however, and admitted that the experience of participating in our Circle of Love program prompted him to resume reading to his daughters, aged nine and twelve. These are difficult ages for young girls to maintain a close relationship with their father, compounded in this case by the extensive traveling required by this man's work. Choosing books from the library, and reading from them to the girls on evenings when he was home, became a warm method of building and strengthening the connection between father and daughters.

Everyone we invited to join our Circle of Love, from parents and police officers to the mayor, the president of General Motors of Canada, bankers, politicians, school board officials, and the chief of police, responded with enthusiasm. We also encouraged older students to read to younger children, nurturing a parenting skill in the older kids at an early age. It was one more way we hoped to break the cycle of parenting problems repeating themselves generation after generation.

We began with readings in the school library every two weeks, and it was such a delight to watch the children snuggle up to these partners, their eyes wide and shining, while they listened to the stories. It was especially dramatic when the person reading to them was a male business executive, or a policeman in full uniform. We welcomed men from our community because the South Simcoe neighbourhood had a high percentage of single-parent families. The majority of our single parents happened to be mothers, and this left many of the boys in our school without good male role models in their lives. We wanted the boys to see men assuming a fathering role, taking time from their business or careers to read stories and chat with children, showing the children they were important. The presence of the men could never, of course, take the place of an absent father or stem abuse from their mother's live-in boyfriend. But it was important nevertheless.

Among the male role models who proved especially popular with the children was one of the tallest uniformed police officers I had ever encountered. Colin Shaw stood well over six feet and arrived at the school in full regalia, including handcuffs, sidearm and billy club, and actually stretched himself full-length on the floor to read aloud to the children. In the beginning they couldn't resist peppering him with questions about his weapon, his handcuffs, and if he had ever appeared on the TV show *Cops*. As time passed, however, they grew more relaxed around Colin. They loved to wear his hat, and the conversations they shared with him extended to include music, fashions, sports, movies—all the diversions important to children yet rarely discussed with adults, let alone a uniformed police officer. Eventually the students didn't seem to notice the uniform at all.

Colin began visiting the school regularly to chat with children, often arriving in his police cruiser. Several months earlier the sight of a police cruiser parked at the school signalled bad news to the children and their parents, who assumed someone was in trouble with the law. Now the sight of a cruiser produced little more than a shrug of the shoulders and the observation, "It's probably just the police reading to the children."

And it almost always was.

Later, the circle expanded beyond the school. We held several sessions at local shopping malls, where we invited children from other schools to join us to listen to stories read to them by the mayor and chief of police.

We welcomed surprise visitors to our Circle of Love from all walks of life, and from all sources. When Curt Tingley, one of our community partners, encountered cartoonist and author Ben Wicks at an airport lounge and described our program to him, Ben agreed to visit us, reading to the students, drawing cartoons and often exaggerating his Cockney accent for comic effect.

Success truly does breed success. With the passage of time, word spread of our achievements, and of the growing number of local businesses and community organizations participating with us in educating the children. This encouraged others to join in, and while we welcomed offers of assistance from every source, we first confirmed that the new partner agreed to abide by our guiding principles. These were:

- Every human being has the right to be respected and the responsibility to respect others.
- Every human being is unique and has a contribution to make.
- Every human being has strengths, which must be nurtured and supported.
- Service to others performed with caring and love makes a difference.

We were grateful for all the involvement that was pledged to us, but I remember we were especially touched by the assistance received from the owner of a small pizza parlour near the school. The young franchise owner was among the first to offer his help, and I was amazed that he was not only an enthusiastic supporter but that he even found time to spend with the children. The pizza store was not a big money-maker for him; he was actually holding down two additional jobs, and he was certainly not a wealthy man. But he believed in the goals we were trying to achieve, and he wanted to give something back to the community. So he visited the school regularly to talk to the children about setting goals, making choices, obtaining an education and the satisfaction of doing a job well, and generally to play the role of a dedicated neighbourhood businessman. He also helped organize Thursday pizza days, paring his profit to the bone to help hungry kids enjoy pizza for lunch one day a week.

The pizza operator's contribution and attitude were one more reason why we declined, with thanks, offers of money to assist the school and its programs. We wanted people to work with us and take ownership of, and responsibility for, the education and well-being of the children. We also wanted them to understand how much we still had to do, and how much help we needed to achieve our goals.

In my third year at South Simcoe, I was so buoyed by the success of our programs and community partnership strategy that I proposed we become even more active, vocal and visible. And what, I asked, is more active, vocal and visible than a parade of children?

We began celebrating the start of each school year with a parade through the neighbourhood as a tribute to our community partners, reinforcing the connection we had established with them. It became, however, a much-needed celebration of the entire community. The school's success was making an impact on the community, and we sought to do more than acknowledge it. We wanted an impossible-to-ignore, in-your-face event that said to the community, *"Don't you just love us??!!"* and defied anyone to disagree.

By this time the school's spirit was so high that the students began choosing names for their classes, linked to the theme of light from the school's motto, *Together We Light the Way*. The names were fun for the kids, who named their classes *The Firecrackers*, *The Flaming Eagles*, *The Shooting Stars* and even the *Kindergarten Kilowatts*. (I suspect this class had some input from the teacher, unless I seriously underestimated the awareness and vocabulary of our kindergarten kids.) The class names were one more step in our effort to build a sense of belonging and connectedness among the students. On one level it was fun to see the high spirits of each class. But on another, deeper level, we knew we were strengthening the connection of the children with the school and with the community. Kids who feel isolated become lost, and kids who feel lost can drift towards problems—poor school work, delinquency, even suicide.

The first parade consisted of the children walking through the neighbourhood, led by school staff. The following year our community partners asked if they could join, and GM provided a truck. Parent Rap members participated, along with Kiwanis and Optimist members who supported our programs. Business mascots such as the Swiss Chalet Chicken, the Kmart Marty, the Shoppers Drug Mart Shutterbug and the Pizza Pizza Doughboy joined in. One way or another, often juggling her busy schedule, the mayor participated as well. The entire procession was led by Constable Colin Shaw in his police cruiser, and the parade became virtually a community-wide event, as impressive as any in the city.

During our parade, each class carried a banner bearing its class name. The children added their own decorative touches, wearing colourful balloons tied to their wrists and singing the school song as they marched, guided by staff and parents. Leading the way, of course, was our mascot Sharkie. Stopping in front of our business partners, the children would repeat the South Simcoe chant while waiting for the manager or owner to emerge. Then two students from each class would hand the proprietor a certificate thanking them for their support and promising to return within a few days to perform a community cleanup around their place of business.

The first stop was always the nearby Legion Hall, where the children assembled in front of the building to be greeted by the manager and his staff. After promising to return over the next few days for a neighbourhood cleanup of trash and garbage, with special attention to the area surrounding the Legion Hall, the children would launch into their chant.

The last line of the chant was delivered in lusty voices and with arms raised in the air, followed by laughter and applause. Then we would move on to greet the next community partner and repeat the process.

Our route was not a long one, because many of the little legs in Grade One couldn't handle a major trek. (The kindergarten classes rode in a school bus decorated with cat whiskers, provided by Laidlaw, one of our community partners.)

New supporters were constantly popping up throughout the community. One day in June, I received a letter from Dr. Frank Gold, a local dentist who occupied an office in the mall across the street. Hearing of our progress at South Simcoe, Dr. Gold congratulated us on the program and expressed a desire to participate. Although we always welcomed new partners, we weren't certain of the potential role for a dentist in the program, and it was too late to accept his services for that school year anyway. In fact we didn't even have time to reply to him before the onset of summer vacation. During our parade in September, however, I got a rather mischievous idea. Instead of drafting a letter to Dr. Gold, thanking him for his offer of support, why not do so in person?

We made a short detour to Dr. Gold's office, assembled outside his door and began chanting his name—"Doctor Gold! Doctor Gold!"—over and over.

The sound of more than 260 voices shouting his name must have alarmed the poor doctor terribly, not to mention the bewildered patient seated in his dental chair. Dr. Gold appeared at the door wearing his white dentist's gown, holding a dental instrument in rubber-gloved hands and wearing an expression of confusion and concern. I quickly explained that we had appreciated his offer of assistance so much that we chose to express our thanks with a visit from the entire school. He broke into a smile while the students applauded and cheered him, then excused himself to scurry back inside to finish treating his anxious patient.

Dr. Gold became yet another active partner in the programs at South Simcoe, and eventually confessed that he had been thrilled by our impetuous visit.

Most schools launched each new school year with a Meet the Teacher event. By our third year Meet the Teacher no longer seemed appropriate because so many individuals from outside the school were involved in the teaching/learning process, including a large number of parents, business and community partners, and special guests such as the mayor and local celebrities.

Instead of Meet the Teacher night, we renamed the event the South Simcoe Community Get-Together, held in the school playground following our parade. The Get-Together was our opportunity to forge relationships around a common cause, and it evolved into something close to a large family picnic. We dined on hot dogs and hamburgers provided by our friends at Swiss Chalet and barbecued by Kiwanis members, and drank iced tea and lemonade. Pony rides and jumping toys in the playground kept the children occupied and burned off excess energy, and the entire area was decorated with balloons and banners honouring our business and community partners.

Our Community Get-Togethers served many purposes. They provided a gathering time for everyone taking ownership of the education of the students; they recognized the support of our community and business partners; and they celebrated our past achievements while setting the stage for new ones in the coming year.

By this time even minor disasters were unable to spoil our success. For our first Community Get-Together, two teachers were assigned to light the barbecues and begin cooking hamburgers and hot dogs. The day was unusually windy, however, and neither teacher was able to get the barbecues lit.

Kim Hutchinson sprang into action. Seizing a cooler filled with raw hamburgers and sprinting across the street to the Swiss Chalet restaurant, she explained the situation to our friend Phil Lawson, and without a moment's hesitation he said, "Leave it to me."

We still don't know how he managed to cook so many hamburgers so quickly, in a kitchen equipped to broil chicken. As many patrons waited patiently for their broiled-chicken dinners, delayed by our hamburgers and hot dogs, Kim entertained them with stories of the accomplishments of South Simcoe students, adding that the children were very hungry and waiting patiently for their lunch. It worked; when Kim sprinted out the door with the cooked hamburgers, several diners actually applauded!

A few months later, when Swiss Chalet announced it would be adding hamburgers to its menu, we jokingly remarked that this minor revolution in corporate policy must have been launched during our Community Get-Together in South Simcoe.

One morning in early November, several children came running to me before classes began, obviously distressed. "There's a fire down the street!" they announced. "And it's in the house where some of our kids live!" The blaze was a block away, and after confirming that the children were safe and it would be unnecessary to evacuate the school, I investigated the circumstances. Three children, recently enrolled in the school, resided in the house. We discovered them, along with their distraught mother and a baby in diapers and a thin blanket, seated in a van nearby. It happened to be a bitterly cold day, and we could either wait for one of the social agencies to arrive or take charge ourselves. Jacki and I put our heads together and decided to take charge.

We went out to the van, met the family, carried the baby inside and made the mother some hot tea. Then we found a warm blanket and oversized woollen socks for the baby, and calmed the family as much as we could. The parents needed to talk with fire authorities, arrange for new accommodations, find a kennel for the family dog and reassure concerned relatives. We told them to leave the children, including the baby, with us.

Meanwhile, the other students began expressing their concern. The president of the Students' Council approached me and proposed a meeting to discuss assisting the family. I agreed, and watched while they assumed leadership and outlined the family's needs. "They have just had a real loss," the Students' Council president pointed out. "They are frightened and don't know if anything is left at their house. So what can we do?"

Their response was wonderful. The senior students took charge, demonstrating all the leadership skills we had taught them. They brainstormed ideas until lunchtime, and many returned from lunch with food, clothing and, best of all, ideas.

Someone pointed out that it wouldn't be fair for the

older child, a girl, to miss classes because she needed to care for the baby. "Let's take turns babysitting," another proposed, and they quickly established a schedule. The rest of the day passed quietly, with the children constantly inquiring about the family's situation and, I realized, enjoying their role as a collective hero. Meanwhile, I felt as though I were about to burst with pride. The children had reacted immediately to the situation. They took the initiative, assumed leadership roles and accepted responsibility with the confidence of individuals twice their age.

As things turned out, the mother was unable to return to retrieve the children until almost six o'clock that evening. I sent the rest of the staff home and remained alone at the school for two hours after the end of classes, playing the roles of principal, babysitter and fill-in mother. It seemed the three children were everywhere at once, keeping me busy changing diapers, offering reassurances and tidying things up while they demonstrated their energy and curiosity. Ah, the life of a public school principal . . .

Not surprisingly, both parents became exceptionally strong supporters of the school and its programs. More gratifying to me, however, was the manner in which the children responded to others in need, just as the community had responded to them earlier. During that one-day crisis we saw the children of South Simcoe rise to the occasion. They began looking out for each other, spontaneously and with love. There was no "What's in it for me?" attitude. Something simply needed to be accomplished by them. And it was.

Look what we've done, I reflected in the days following the fire. Together, the school and community had fostered changes that would have been unimaginable a few years earlier. At one point the students of South Simcoe Public School had been considered the source of problems in the neighbourhood. Now they were self-confident, loving and caring children, who generated pride and affection among all who encountered them.

Especially their principal.

Chapter 11

From Worst to First

By our third year of implementing programs at South Simcoe, word of our success began to spread beyond the neighbourhood and the city of Oshawa. In the fall of 1994, I was surprised to receive a call from the Canadian Broadcasting Corporation, which was dedicating an episode of their award-winning *Man Alive* television series to the subject of resilient children. The network dispatched crews from Toronto to visit schools all across Canada in search of the most outstanding programs for building resilience in kids. When they arrived in Edmonton to discuss the project with Steve Ramsanker, he was amazed to see them. "Why did you travel all this way," Steve asked them, "when you have a wonderful example right in your own backyard, in Oshawa?"

For almost five weeks we shared the school with TV cameras, lights, sound equipment and TV crew members, as they captured our daily routine and ventured into some students' homes to interview parents and children.

The show aired across Canada early in 1995, and within a day or two I received a telephone call from Jennifer, an executive with General Motors of Canada. GM was looking for someone from outside the automotive industry to discuss leadership principles at a marketing conference attended by managers from the company's Ontario zone. One condition, they asked, was that I avoid any kind of formal presentation—no notes, no charts, no overhead projection materials. "Just be prepared to field questions," Jennifer suggested.

I was concerned about my ability to make a presentation under those circumstances, but my nervousness quickly dissipated when the 150 GM managers rose to their feet and applauded as I entered the conference room. The time flew past, quickly and easily. What's more, the audience seemed genuinely pleased with, and surprised at, my answers to their questions, and proved it with thunderous applause at the end.

Afterwards, Jennifer asked if they could do anything for me in return—a monetary contribution to the school, perhaps?

"It would be easy for you to write a cheque," I replied. "But money is not the most valuable thing you can contribute. The school needs to see evidence of long-term involvement from people like you and your colleagues. We need you to visit the school, work with our students and spend time with them."

My suggestion unleashed an outpouring of new support from the people in GM's Ontario zone. Jennifer McDonald and Barry Kuntz and their staff joined our Circle of Love program, arriving regularly to read aloud to the children, eventually participating in our Triple-S and Connections programs as well.

Then something extraordinary happened. When Jennifer and Barry saw our programs in action, witnessed the children setting and achieving goals, and studied the affirmations displayed throughout the school, they asked if they could bring several Ontario-zone employees with them on their next visit. Fascinated by our achievements, they were especially interested in the way we interacted as a team. They wanted to observe us in action, unveiling whatever "magic formula" we had managed to create, and apply it to their own work activities. We agreed, of course, and watched as our visitors grew intrigued by our shared leadership, our focus on setting goals and reflecting on them at the end of each day, our creation of a trusting and caring environment, and our emphasis on smiling at each other—staff and students alike.

They noted with interest the way we always spoke of strengths and areas for growth and development, never of weaknesses and deficiencies, and they marvelled at our ability to achieve so much with so few material assets. They appreciated our refusal to focus on things we did not have and our insistence on emphasizing the resources we owned. They also praised our Bouquet Board, where staff members wrote compliments to each other.

Many of these ideas found their way into GM training programs, and when other GM zones grew aware of the lessons to be learned from South Simcoe, they invited me to speak to their groups as well. As a result I travelled to B.C.'s beautiful Okanagan Valley, to Calgary, to Prince Edward Island and to Winnipeg. The warmth of the hospitality in Winnipeg countered the January weather, as did viewing the *Man Alive* segment on South Simcoe, which was projected on a giant IMAX screen. At each location I asked my audience to participate in a Circle of Love reading program in their area. "Children need to know they are valued by people like you," I repeated. "You *can* work with me and make a difference!"

What an amazing development! South Simcoe Public School, located in the heart of Oshawa's inner city, was teaching important lessons to a division of one of the world's largest, most dynamic corporations. It put an entirely new spin on the idea of "giving something back to the community."

Community support at its best is a two-way street, with each side taking turns at giving and receiving. We were proud that Barry, Frank and other members of their team at GM valued our school as a source of management and teamwork training ideas. And we were gratified when they and other GM employees helped us turn a potentially tragic Christmas into a joyous event one year.

It concerned Penny and her children. Penny, a single mother struggling valiantly to better herself and her children, had become a strong advocate for our programs at the school. A regular participant in Parent Rap sessions, Penny had moved out of the neighbourhood in search of better living conditions, yet insisted on her children continuing to attend our school because of the relationships they had built. She and her family shared an apartment with a second family that included two teenaged boys.

With only mother's allowance as her income, Penny managed to set aside enough money each week that, in mid-December, she was able to purchase some food treats and a few gifts for her children to enjoy at Christmas. The holiday season meant a great deal to Penny, and she looked forward to seeing the smiles on the faces of her children on Christmas Day. They would open their gifts in the morning and share what would be for them a somewhat elaborate meal that evening.

But it was not to be. A week before Christmas the other family's teenaged boys raided the freezer, ate most of Penny's food and tossed out whatever they were unable to consume. Then they stole the gifts Penny had wrapped and hidden for her children, selling them on the street for money to play video games.

Penny was devastated. Life, which had been hard for her for so many years, had turned cruelly unfair. No mother's allowance cheques would arrive before Christmas. There would be no presents for her children, no modest feast, and very little joy.

Jacki Devolin heard of Penny's situation and passed the news on to me. Could we do anything to help the family? It didn't look very promising. All our normal sources of assistance at Christmas had already given to needy families; it was unfair to call them now, so close to the holiday. In quiet desperation I called Frank at General Motors, and quickly explained the situation to him.

He recognized my description of Penny almost immediately. "Wasn't she in the *Man Alive* show?" he asked.

I told him she was indeed.

"A lot of people around here saw that broadcast and were moved by it," he said. "And some heard you speak here. I don't know what I can do on short notice, but I'll try my best."

What he did was virtually miraculous. When word spread throughout the GM zone offices where I had spoken, we became almost inundated with a small avalanche of cheques and cash donations to be used for Penny. In fact, we received enough money to replace the food and gifts stolen from Penny and also help a second family in distress.

Over the Christmas break I recalled the warm generosity of our new GM partners many times. We can count on them, I realized. They have become part of the extended family we have put together. When we have a need, when we are in trouble, we can count on them for support, no questions asked. Just as if they were family.

What a wonderful discovery to make at that time of the year.

Barry had heard someone in GM's Ontario zone refer to our school as "the Saturn of the education world," meaning of course the innovative and non-conforming approach of GM's Saturn division.

I was thinking of that remark when I spoke at a celebration of the school's eightieth birthday a few weeks later. Over six hundred visitors crowded the school and grounds, overflowing from the classrooms into the halls, and out of the halls onto the playground. I mentioned the comparison during my talk. "Actually," I quipped, "Saturn is the South Simcoe of the automotive industry."

We both made our points.

The CBC *Man Alive* segment was shown on a number of occasions, and the day following a repeat telecast someone commented that our story would make an ideal feature for *Reader's Digest* magazine. "If it's meant to happen, it will," I said.

Obviously, it *was* meant to happen. The previous evening a woman in Kamloops, B.C., named Lynn Schuyler was having difficulty dropping off to sleep and thought perhaps a few minutes staring at her TV set might make her drowsy. What she began watching did not make her drowsy at all. It was the *Man Alive* telecast, and instead of preparing her for bed, the show alerted her to a perfect story idea for *Reader's Digest.* The next morning Lynn began tracking me down, contacting me barely two hours after my off-the-cuff response to the idea of a *Reader's Digest* article on South Simcoe. When Lynn introduced herself and the reason for her call, I burst into laughter. I have always believed that, if you are on the right path, the right things will happen. Not surprisingly, Lynn's telephone call cemented that belief more firmly than ever in my heart.

I was also invited to make an appearance on the CBC's immensely popular radio show *Morningside*, hosted by Peter Gzowski. Peter, besides being perhaps the best-known media celebrity in the country at the time, is also a strong advocate of literacy education. As the interview progressed, he grew more and more enthusiastic and supportive. "Tell me what you might need at the school," he said near the close of our talk.

I asked him what he meant.

"We're being heard coast to coast across Canada right now," he said. "If there is something you and the school can use for your program, go ahead and ask for it."

I mentioned two things. Photographs, I explained, played a large role in our work at the school; we displayed photos of the children and their successes throughout the school, and wanted to expand the program if possible.

Almost immediately, CBC received a call from Anne Hartling, marketing manager for Colortron, a photo shop in Stoney Creek, near Hamilton, Ontario. Anne was so supportive of our work that she not only offered film and photo finishing, but also visited the school, along with colleagues Sue and Steve, to teach the basics of photography to the children.

The students learned how to take photos, process the prints, and mount them for display, and this enabled us to launch a program in which the children took photographs of things in the world around them that made them happy. It proved to be a wonderful project, made possible by Anne's generosity.

I also mentioned how badly we needed a bus from time to time, for excursions. We wanted the children of South Simcoe, many of whom had never travelled beyond their own city limits, to discover other nearby sites like Toronto and Niagara Falls.

"Anybody out there got a bus?" Peter said. "Sandra Dean needs a bus!"

A few days later someone who had been listening to the radio suggested I call one of our partners, the Tim Horton donut chain. Sure enough, they were pleased to make their bus available for excursions, and later that school year our students were visiting historic sites aboard a luxury air-conditioned bus thanks to Tim Horton Donuts and Peter Gzowski.

Professor Bob Ellis, associate dean at the School of Business at Wilfrid Laurier University, asked permission to do a case study on leadership. He later told me that this case was a favourite with his students.

The *Reader's Digest* story was one of a long chain of events that spread the word of our activities far beyond the South Simcoe neighbourhood. Our story spread across Canada, down to the U.S., then overseas to Europe and eventually all the way to Australia. Strangers began stopping staff members on the street to discuss our programs. Mail and telephone calls arrived from more foreign locations than I can remember, and requests for interviews and speeches became so numerous that we were unable to handle them all. The letters became so voluminous, in fact, that I simply placed them in a box in my office until I could find time to read and respond to them. It was reassuring to see such an outpouring of interest, but I refused to let all the attention distract me from my prime duties.

Just a few years earlier I had walked in one direction to seek help from the Legion members and in the other direction looking for assistance from neighbouring mall merchants. Now the traffic had reversed, and as *Together We Light the Way* began making an impact, others were coming to us.

It was nothing less than astonishing.

In all, I appeared on Peter Gzowski's radio show three times, and during the third appearance a woman named Courtney Garneau, working in Communications with the federal Justice Department, happened to hear me discuss our achievements at South Simcoe. School violence was beginning to attract wide media interest in Canada, most of it focused on a "Let's get tough with the kids" approach. Our philosophy, of course, was based on a totally opposite strategy, based upon building trust and self-worth among the children. Intrigued by this, and impressed with our achievements, Courtney telephoned me shortly afterwards and invited me to Ottawa, where I discussed our Respect program, Circle of Love and other activities in some detail. This led, eventually, to the opportunity to expand this program far beyond South Simcoe.

We made enormous progress building relationships with the community, boosting the self-worth of the children and transforming South Simcoe Public School into the heartbeat of the community, a spiritual oasis for all who came there. We had created the foundation of a plan to achieve academic excellence, to be measured by standardized tests in reading, writing and mathematics.

Unfortunately, these tests would not measure aspects such as the emotional stability of the children. We were building resiliency and inner strength in the kids, and we all saw these qualities growing more apparent among the students, but the task of raising a child's reading level by three or four grade levels is never accomplished overnight.

I clung to these thoughts when studying the results of the region's first series of district-wide exams. Ours were dreadful. We lingered at the bottom of the list in every category. If someone were to judge the impact of all our hard work and commitment based on those results alone, they would be appalled. Of the 120 elementary schools in our district, South Simcoe was rated dead last.

In my heart I knew we were on the right track. By every other measure we were making good progress. Class disturbances had been drastically reduced, attendance had increased dramatically, and you could sense an attitude of striving to learn in virtually every class. The children were smiling, confident and articulate, they loved attending school, and they were working hard to prove they belonged at South Simcoe.

The staff and I consoled ourselves with this knowledge. But how would the parents react to the disastrous test results? Would they decide that our noble experiment had failed, that their children were doomed to reside at the bottom of the academic totem pole? Should we even discuss the results at the next Parent Rap session? Perhaps we could avoid the subject entirely and hope the question never arose.

We decided to meet the issue head-on. At the next Parent Rap, I presented the results to the parents and awaited their response. To their everlasting credit, every parent stated flatly that they didn't care about the results of the district-wide exams.

"We know how hard you and your staff are working," one parent said, "and we can see that our kids are learning. Just look at them."

"My son is reading, and he used to hate reading," another added. "Now he enjoys it. He's even showing off how well he can read. So what if he's not at the Grade Three level yet? The way he's going, I know he'll be there by the end of the year."

Our efforts to build relationships with the parents, by taking time to explain our strategies and ask for their support, were paying off. They had become advocates of the school and of our approach to raising the students' level of self-worth. It was a heartwarming response, and I left the session feeling more confident than ever that we were making a difference to both the children and their parents. We had raised the school's pride and confidence; now we had to raise its academic levels to similar levels. But how?

I have always hated the term "strengths and weaknesses." If you honestly believe in the concept of lifelong learning, how can you accept the term "weakness"? In educational terms we suffer no weaknesses; we simply recognize areas for new growth and development. The solution to enhancing the school's academic levels was in our school motto, *Together We Light the Way*, and in our guiding principles: the right to be respected, the precious value of children, the importance of making them feel loved and safe, and the recognition that every human being is unique with a role to play in life.

There is always a way. If we work together, we will find it.

We gradually restored our confidence by strengthening the programs and activities already in place, and even adding a few new ones. We produced a booklet on our Triple-S program, and began work on a similar guide to our Connections program. Our Circle of Love reading schedule was swinging into high gear, to the delight of both the children and the adults reading to them. Business people and educators alike were asking us to share our ideas and methods with them, and our Parent Rap members were being invited to visit other schools, where they explained the operation and benefits of our programs.

We also took comfort in the continuing support from officials at the board, who understood that elevating our academic levels would not be an overnight miracle. They knew we were making progress and, as a reflection of their belief in our programs, some members persuaded us to apply for an award from the Conference Board of Canada. These awards, presented each year to recognize partnerships between schools and business, were highly prized and hotly contested by schools all across the country. If South Simcoe Public School could win recognition in that forum, it would go a long way in assuaging our disappointment over the poor academic results.

With the encouragement and financial support of my director and superintendents, I attended that year's Conference Board event and returned filled with enthusiasm and resolve. Our programs, I was convinced, stood a good chance of being selected for recognition at the next event. This wasn't simply my own personal evaluation but the opinion of others, who encouraged me to continue the programs and submit an entry the following year.

All of this activity, together with the day-to-day demands

of my role as principal, were taking a toll on my energy. The truth is, I was growing mentally and physically exhausted. Between acting as principal, supervising programs, maintaining contacts with our community partners and conducting media interviews, my work had become a seemingly endless procession of meetings, discussions and decision-making. I was usually loving every bit of it, but even happy work can be too much for one person. I was paying a price for the long hours and weekend work, even if I refused to admit it.

That summer, both Ishwar and the boys insisted that I take an extended vacation in Trinidad. I had returned to Trinidad frequently to visit family and friends, who were unfailing in their pride in my accomplishments and their encouragement. But this trip was somewhat special. I spent long hours in conversation with people who had helped shape my values as a child, and the experience was truly a spiritual renewal. Then Ishwar and I went to Tobago, where we had spent our honeymoon so many years earlier, and I whiled away many long, languid days soaking up sunshine, catching up on my sleep, walking on the beaches and generally recharging my batteries.

When I returned to begin the new school year, I discovered a new reservoir of energy, and I applied it towards raising our academic levels to match our other achievements. More than ever, I saw our community partnerships as a special extended family, capable of providing spiritual sustenance to the children just as my family and friends back in Trinidad had provided for me. I grew determined to shine our light so brightly that no one could ignore it.

We began to document our programs and successes in preparation for the Conference Board of Canada's Award for

Excellence in Business and Education Partnerships. From the first day of school in September, with the invaluable help of Pauline Langmaid, a board facilitator, and Tamara Gattie, one of our teachers, we described our procedures, recorded our achievements and evaluated our findings, assisted along the way by people at the board office who wanted us to succeed.

Then, near disaster. On the day we were to courier our presentation to the Conference Board for arrival the following day, we realized that some of the information on the application was inadequate. Rewriting meant missing the one-thirty courier pickup, but I refused to send an inadequate presentation, so we set to work on major revisions. The next pickup time was five-thirty, but by mid-afternoon we realized we wouldn't make that one either. Another company agreed to pick up the presentation at nine o'clock, and we worked through the dinner hour, by now practically staggering with exhaustion. Still the work went on, and we had to cancel even that late-hour courier, finally settling on a company that promised same-day delivery for a hefty fee.

We found the money and somehow also found the energy to wrap things up at eleven o'clock that evening. By that time my entire body was so weary that I couldn't even put my contacts back in, and the arrival of the courier service was, quite literally, a sight for sore eyes.

We had worked so hard, and now everything was in the hands of strangers who, I prayed, would see our programs not as some optimistic "love-in" but as a serious, multi-faceted and measured effort to reach goals many others had once considered impossible.

The call arrived in February. Tiny South Simcoe Public School, the school that had sat at the very bottom of the

Durham board test results one year earlier, had been declared the best of all Ontario's elementary and secondary schools in the competition for Excellence in Business and Education Partnerships sponsored by the Conference Board of Canada.

We whooped, we hugged and we laughed. Then I shared the news with the school over the PA system, which set off such an explosion of cheering by the students that I wondered if it could be heard ten miles away, at the school board offices. I followed this up with visits to each classroom, where I explained in detail the meaning of the recognition and why they should feel proud, because the award was more theirs than anyone's.

The eventual winner would be chosen from among the regional winners at the formal presentation, which was to be held in Saint John, New Brunswick, later in the spring, and this posed a problem. The Conference Board would make travel arrangements for me to attend, but I felt it would be terribly unfair if I were the only representative from the school to attend the awards ceremony. None of our achievements would have been possible without hard work and sacrifice by the staff and the support of our partners; they deserved to share the honour and recognition. A team effort had won the award, and a team should be on hand to receive it.

In a meeting with Pauline Laing, my director, I explained my dilemma and made an impulsive promise. "If you can arrange to make time available for the teachers to attend," I said, "I'll arrange the rest." Meaning, of course, the expense of flying our entire staff to New Brunswick.

Pauline came to the rescue. If the parents agreed, a Professional Development Day could be shifted, providing the time needed. The parents enthusiastically supported the idea. Now it was time to raise the money to cover travel and accommodation.

The community support was nothing less than inspirational. When word spread that we needed funds to send the staff to New Brunswick, parents and trustees went to work, and soon contributions of five, ten and twenty-five dollars began arriving, along with congratulations and fervent beliefs that we would be selected best in the country. Substantial amounts came from surprising sources: the neighbouring Kmart, where a few years earlier some of our students were considered rampant shoplifters, sent a thousand dollars, while Mike, our school trustee, drummed up support from the entire board and even convinced Doug Ross, another trustee, to contribute five hundred dollars.

We invited all our partners to attend, including members of the police force, and the chief of police responded by sending Colin Shaw and his partner in a brand-new police van to drive the nine hundred kilometres from Oshawa to Saint John.

The event was much more than an awards ceremony. Each regional winner set up booths and displays in a conference hall where over six hundred attendees, most of them educators, milled about looking at photographs, examining records and chatting with representatives at the booths. Constable Shaw helped at our booth, which drew a few curious comments from visitors, who may have thought a uniformed police officer was a necessary player in all our activities.

Everyone seemed intrigued by our programs and impressed with our accomplishments. They loved the photographs of the children we used to decorate the booth (provided by Steve and Sue at Colortron), and they were impressed by the partnerships we had forged among members of the community. Still, none of us dared to hope that we might be chosen the winner among all the schools in Canada.

Then the moment for the formal announcement arrived. We held our breath . . . crossed our fingers . . . then erupted in more joy and noise than I ever expected a small group of teachers and two police officers could express.

When the pandemonium settled down, I wanted everyone who supported us back home to hear the news. The school board, I knew, was holding an evening meeting at the board office. We had to call them and share the excitement. But no one was at the building's main switchboard at that late hour. There was simply no way to get the word to the meeting room—until Constable Colin Shaw said, "Leave it to me." He called police headquarters back in Oshawa and had a police cruiser dispatched, complete with flashing lights, to the board office, where the officer managed to rouse someone who admitted him to the meeting room with the good news.

I have always wished in a small way that I had been present that evening when the Durham District School Board, probably deep in a discussion of budgets and curricula, was suddenly interrupted by a police officer arriving with, I'm sure they expected, news of some near or imminent disaster—only to discover that South Simcoe Public School had just won a prestigious national award.

The Conference Board of Canada presentation was not the first award to South Simcoe, but it was the first award made *outside the school system*, which validated the significance of our programs beyond the school walls. It was also our first truly national award as well, and one that recognized our success at doing effective yet simple—*not simplistic*—

things with very little money. A good deal of our success was admittedly a result of persuading our many partners to accept their social responsibility and join us. In other words, we could never have achieved our goals alone. But really—aren't partnership and a sharing of responsibility something that every society should expect from its members?

We tried to accommodate visits from other educators, and several groups began arriving to learn what we were doing and why it seemed to be working so well. My old friend and mentor Ken Leithwood surveyed a number of schools to establish relative levels of enthusiasm among the staff. The results from interviews conducted at South Simcoe, he told me with astonishment, went right off the chart; they were so high that they unfairly skewed data obtained from other schools in the survey. Things had certainly changed since my appointment as principal of South Simcoe Public School just a few years earlier. Now, no staff loved their work more.

The children enjoyed the growing attention being paid to their school. Little Meagan, whose singing voice stirred hearts at every school assembly, seemed to take special pride in welcoming visitors. She would rush to greet them, thrust out a tiny hand and say "Welcome to South Simcoe!" Her positive attitude and her pride in her achievements—it took only the barest hint to encourage Meagan to display her portfolio of work—summed up so much that we had strived to accomplish, and set the tone for many tours by visitors.

It occurred to me that Meagan was unconsciously teaching us a lesson. We all need encouragement, support and assurance that our presence on earth is valued and appreciated, and Meagan needed this as much as anyone. Her family situation prevented her from savouring the joy and satisfaction that comes from being loved and appreciated. Many children react to this kind of situation with rebellion and alienation. But Meagan chose to find acceptance elsewhere, first from the teaching staff, and later from visitors to the school. Some visitors arrived as skeptical strangers, but they usually departed the school totally beguiled by this little girl's enthusiasm and poise.

In August 1995 we were asked to present our programs to a major organization at their annual event in Toronto. (We celebrated by pitching in twenty dollars each and hiring a stretch limousine, complete with uniformed chauffeur, to drive us there and back. On the way we toasted our new celebrity status with non-alcoholic champagne!) Even our now-lovely gardens were attracting attention. The following month South Simcoe was declared the winner of the Looking Good Award, given to the school judged to have the most attractive grounds of all 120 schools in the region.

But good looks, I kept reminding myself, can take you only so far. Our bottom-of-the-barrel rating for reading, writing and mathematics still felt like a millstone around my neck. Two things kept raising my spirits. First, we had no direction to go but up, as I kept repeating to the staff, over and over. And second, I had a sense that we had passed some sort of watershed, that we were gaining momentum, and that our standing in the previous series of board tests did not capture the reality of things at South Simcoe.

The reality, I believed, was that we and the children had made a breakthrough, and the learning curve that had been rising slowly upwards was steadily climbing higher and faster than any of us could measure.

When the Ontario Ministry of Education announced

that it would conduct a provincial standardized test, I could hardly contain my excitement. Sally Roberts and Joanne Blohm, the Grade Three teachers, were confident in the abilities of their students. When the results finally arrived, virtually the entire staff gathered in the staff room to share in the news.

It was amazing.

South Simcoe Public School was no longer at the bottom of the barrel, or even in the middle of the pack. Our results were substantially higher than the average for all elementary schools in the entire province of Ontario. We had managed to rise dramatically in the ratings for reading, writing and mathematics. The gardens, the awards, the recognition and the media coverage all paled in comparison.

Our kids were not only more proud, more confident, more respectful and more articulate than before. They were also outstanding students.

Chapter 12

The Gifts
They Gave Us

*T*hrough 1996, South Simcoe garnered international recognition. Early in that year we were informed that our board of education had been nominated as an entry in a competition to honour excellence in school systems, sponsored by the giant Bertelsmann Foundation of Germany. As a result of this nomination South Simcoe Public School would be added to the tour being conducted by the Bertelsmann judges.

The criteria for the competition required the jury to assess a long list of qualities, including each school system's concern for learning and life chances; originality and evolution; employee potential; innovative school leadership; participation of pupils, parents and other agencies; co-operation between individual schools and external decision-makers; evaluation and quality assurance; and a framework to support similar development on a national level.

We added a few extra touches for the Bertelsmann judges, especially when we learned they had been touring for three months before arriving at South Simcoe. Instead of taking them to a restaurant for a special lunch—we thought they may have consumed too many restaurant meals by this point—we prepared a home-cooked meal and fed them in the school. Alvena baked fresh bread, and its heavenly aroma wafted towards the judges as soon as they entered the building; Jane cooked and served her favourite casserole. We also invited Phil Lawson, our Swiss Chalet partner, and Curt Tingley from General Motors to join us and discuss our programs from the perspective of business people.

Before they began their tour of the classrooms, each judge was provided with a supply of Respect Tickets, and invited to dispense them to students based on the guidelines they heard during our presentation. This proved a very practical way of demonstrating how the program worked, and enabled the judges to witness the glow of pride in the eyes of the students.

We went from classroom to classroom, with the judges growing more impressed by the minute. In Sally Roberts's Grade Four class they inspected the student portfolios and asked one girl to name her best subject.

"Reading," she said without hesitation. "I'm a really good reader."

One member asked how she could tell.

"Easy," the girl replied. "I'll show you."

As the judges watched, she withdrew her portfolio from the desk, opened it up, and showed them pages that illustrated her level of reading in September and her current level. The girl had progressed three years in reading levels in less than one year, and she demonstrated it with poise and pride.

Downstairs in the kindergarten class, Nancy was reading a story to the children when the judges entered. After the judges introduced themselves, one asked the children if they were proud of their school. "Yes!" the children responded, almost rattling the windows with their voices.

"You show them," Nancy suggested to the class, and the youngsters spontaneously exploded in the loudest, most enthusiastic South Simcoe chant ever delivered by a group of five year olds.

At the end of the tour the jury members expressed their surprise and pleasure at the staff's enthusiasm and dedication, and at the confidence and pride of the students. They also went on to praise the consistency of our programming. "In every classroom," one of them commented, "from kindergarten to Grade Eight, the teachers and students understand their goals, and can describe them accurately and consistently. Most important, they are achieving their goals."

The judges were impressed—so impressed that a film crew arrived from Germany in May to spend two days filming at our school, and an additional two days at Sinclair Secondary School, the "showcase school" for the award. The presence of the film crew was evidence that we had done more than simply impress the Bertelsmann judges, and in September it was made official: Durham District School Board, represented by Sinclair Secondary School with South Simcoe Public School also showcased, had won out over school systems in Hungary, New Zealand, Norway, Scotland and Switzerland to be declared the best, most innovative school system in the world.

During an International Partnership Conference, for which South Simcoe acted as a host school, I watched as one member, a dour Norwegian, moved through the school without exhibiting any apparent response to all that he saw and heard. I feared he actually disapproved of our programs, but later that year, when I encountered him at an educational conference in Calgary, I learned that he had, in fact, been very impressed. I also discovered he was head of the Norwegian Confederation of Business and Industry. As a result of his visit and that meeting I was invited to make the keynote address at their international partnership conference in Norway the following summer.

Other invitations began arriving from international destinations. I was delighted to be invited by the Royal Bank in Trinidad and Tobago to return to my home country, where I spoke about the development of business and educational partnerships. Prime Minister Basdeo Panday opened the event and, needless to say, the experience was immensely flattering and moving to me. In many ways it was like coming home, and enabled me to reach back to my roots, the region and the culture that had shaped me. Shortly afterwards, Dr. Keith Mitchell, prime minister of Grenada, who had attended my session at the International Partnership Conference, invited me to Grenada to launch a partnership initiative with school principals, teachers and business people. I made several visits to Grenada to do this, and during this time, the prime minister's first annual awards for excellence in partnership were held. During the ceremonies, I had the opportunity to also address the prime ministers of other Caribbean nations. Shortly afterwards I set off for Jamaica upon an invitation by Bill Clarke, head of Scotia Bank, to speak to bank managers at their conference there.

Later I was given the opportunity to visit South Africa, where my keynote address to a conference centred on the importance of community support in children's education. The people I met in South Africa, where there is such hunger for knowledge and so few resources to provide it, were thrilled to hear the message that *Together We Can Light the Way*. They needed to know that a small school facing many challenges in far-off Canada had succeeded in forging programs for itself. If we could do it, I assured them, they could as well. I stressed the need to work with children and help them find their strengths, and having found them, to encourage the students to develop and apply their skills with support from partners in their community. "Not support from the wallets," I emphasized. "Support from the hearts."

I explained how a large number of people, each giving just a little of their time, can make an enormous impact on the lives of children. I talked of the critical need to teach respect for self and others, and the value of teamwork and initiative. I described the struggles faced by children such as Melanie, Meagan, Bobby, Leonard, Cathy, Barbara and so many others we had encountered, and how we helped them cope with the challenges they faced while developing skills and growing more resilient. I underlined the concept of kids and communities learning and growing together, and the importance of having someone believe in kids until the children acquired the inner strength to believe in themselves. I assured my listeners that they should begin making positive choices and finding their own paths, and not wait for someone else to do it for them. "If we change the way people *think* about themselves and about others," I repeated time after time, "we can change the way they *act* towards themselves and others. Then the world becomes a better place."

One day in the spring of 1998, I returned home from school as usual and checked my voice mail system. All but one were the familiar kinds of messages, spoken in familiar voices by people with familiar names.

One was anonymous. I could not recognize the voice. "Sandra," it said, "I'm someone who cares about South Simcoe school, and I want you to know this. The school is going to be closed. I don't want you to be shocked by the news, because I know you have said that it would only close over your dead body."

That was all. They hung up.

I felt as though I had been kicked in the stomach.

It could have been just a crank call. Who would leave a message like that without mentioning their name? But the words had been delivered with such authority that I knew they were true. Due to budget restraints, school boards everywhere were being forced to reassess the economics of operating buildings that were small and costly to maintain.

Like South Simcoe.

I mentioned the telephone call to no one at the school.

A few days later, when I was at the board offices, hoping against hope that the rumour was untrue, Grant Yeo, my director, called me into his office for a chat. He closed the door behind us and I knew instinctively what he was going to say.

"We're going to be announcing the closure of your school," he said in a solemn yet kind and caring voice, like a physician announcing the death of a relative. "I want to handle this in a manner that won't create a negative impact on the community, and I need your co-operation."

Thanks to the anonymous telephone call, I managed to remain calm while he explained that, in a sweeping cost-cutting plan, the Durham District School Board would be closing eleven old schools, most of them in heavily urbanized areas, and constructing twelve new schools in developing neighbourhoods.

It was not something anyone wanted to do, but every possible way of keeping the school open had been explored. There was no real alternative. Grant encouraged me to look on the bright side of things. I had always despaired that South Simcoe lacked a gymnasium, a large library and sufficient washrooms. Moving the children to a newer, larger school would provide them with all of these facilities.

I tried, but I simply couldn't accept the closing of South Simcoe as a step forward for the children.

Things grew worse when, soon after my talk with the director, I had to sit through a meeting and listen as someone read aloud the names of all the schools to be closed. Through the list they went, moving closer to the revelation that I knew was coming but found difficult to acknowledge, and when they reached "South Simcoe Public School," it was as though someone plunged a knife into my heart. I sat frozen in my chair. I may have been a dedicated educational professional and a member of this important and influential group, but I was blinking back tears. How could this be the fate of a school that had been praised as a beacon of hope for other schools, and as a spiritual oasis for the entire community?

When the meeting finally ended, I managed to rise from my chair, walk to my car, drive the long distance back to the school and break the sad news to the staff.

By this time, I had resigned myself to reality. Drawing on my leadership training, I began concentrating on ways to help the staff and students deal with the news. At the school I found myself taking the official board position, explaining the logic of its decision to the hardest-working, most dedicated group of teachers I had ever been privileged to know, while they dabbed tissues at their eyes or stared blankly into space.

"This is not entirely unexpected," I pointed out. "We have done wonderful things here, and made a difference to so many kids. Unfortunately, the building is old, it is inefficient to operate, and there is no room for expansion on the lot to accommodate a gymnasium and other things we need." I asked them to remember the importance of working together to make the change as easy as possible for the children.

In June, the day before our Community Day and the celebration of the school's eighty-second anniversary, the decision was made public. At the end of the next school year South Simcoe Public School would be closed and shuttered, left to await demolition or sale. The press practically stormed the school in the middle of the festivities, with five TV stations dispatching cameras and reporters to cover the story. Fortunately, I had anticipated the media response. Ann Hartling and Linda Sinclair helped me prepare a statement regarding the closing of the school, and I read it over and over again to reporters and interviewers throughout the day. The joy of the celebration, of course, dissolved in the reality of the school's imminent closing.

That's one reason I remember that day so vividly. The other reason? It was the only time in all my years at South Simcoe that we had rain on the school's Community Day.

With the word now made official, I personally visited each class, explaining to the children that they deserved better facilities than we were able to provide at South Simcoe. It was a fine old building, but its time had passed. "Nobody enjoys closing a school," I said, "least of all its principal." Least of all *this* principal, I might have added.

And that October, in the midst of a beautiful autumn, the final autumn in the final year for South Simcoe Public School, a remarkable thing happened.

Once again the board had conducted exams to determine abilities in reading, writing and mathematics among Grade Three students in all 120 schools composing the district. This time we didn't open the results with the same breathless excitement as before; but we were stunned, nevertheless. The findings were clear and unequivocal: South Simcoe students were performing at the top two levels in reading and mathematics, and 94 percent of our Grade Three students achieved the top two levels in reading, writing and mathematics skills. South Simcoe was no longer merely above average in its academic performance; on the basis of these tests it was the most successful inner-city school in the province.

There was more.

According to the report, a remarkably high percentage of South Simcoe students attended school regularly and promptly, and the overwhelming majority of our Grade Seven and Grade Eight students earned at least two A's on their report card. Once notorious for incidents of vandalism and shoplifting, the report noted, South Simcoe now enjoyed the steady support of twenty-six business partners and community agencies. And the school that once could entice only three parents to each Parent Rap session now drew at least one out of every four parents to its meetings.

Upon hearing the news of the school's closing, some of these same parents resolved to save the building. Their presentations, letters to the editors of local newspapers and outraged telephone calls to local politicians all repeated the same theme: How could they close a school that had won the national award from the Conference Board of Canada? They can't just shut down a school that had done so much for so many in the South Simcoe neighbourhood.

Well, they could, and they did.

Towards the end of 1998 I had accepted the decision intel-
lectually, if not emotionally, and was determined to handle
the situation with as much grace and decorum as I could
muster. Still, it seemed as though irony kept piling atop
irony.

During the same week in December 1998 that the decision to close South Simcoe Public School was declared bind-
ing and irrevocable, the federal justice department
announced a spending commitment of $1.8 million to fund
the extension of our programs to schools all across the country, along with a contribution from the Ontario Ministry of
Education and Training. This was announced at a Triple-S
ceremony, conducted in the Legion Hall and attended by a
host of federal members of parliament and members of the
provincial legislature, plus several business and community
partners. This was a huge celebration. Every staff member,
every student and every interested parent we could squeeze
into the hall was invited to attend. I reminded each class that
they had not only helped themselves by participating in our
programs at South Simcoe; they had also provided models
for others all over the world.

I was asked to head the justice department's initiative to
be called "Building Stronger and Safer Communities Using
the *Together We Light the Way* Model." Yes, *Together We Light
the Way* was now a model. The work we had done, and the
lessons we had learned, could now make a difference to
untold numbers of children everywhere in Canada. We had
helped make a difference to an entire community; now I
could perhaps help to make a difference to an entire country, and even beyond Canada.

The ministry's description of our program, as contained
in a news release of December 16, 1998, managed to sum up

all that we had conceived, refined and practiced over the previous seven years:

> Together We Light the Way . . . *is a school-based inter-*
> *vention model that builds resiliency and responsibility in*
> *young children and relies on the commitment of teachers,*
> *parents and the community for its success. The model reduces*
> *risk factors affecting young children and increases protective*
> *factors.*

Why would the Ministry of Justice make use of our
program? Because

> *the elementary school setting provides perhaps the only*
> *consistent access to large numbers of children.*

My final day at South Simcoe fell immediately before
the Christmas vacation period. During my years at South
Simcoe we maintained a tradition at the school of "clapping
out" Grade Eights who were moving on to high school. On
their final day at the school the Grade Eights would walk
along the lower corridor, which was lined with all the other
students. As the senior students moved towards the door for
their final exit, the remaining students would shake their
hands and applaud them. This was our "clap out," and it
proved so moving and popular that some Grade Eights
would exit and scurry around to re-enter the school from
the other side, just to be "clapped out" again.

I had always dreamed of leaving in the same manner.
But it would be both inappropriate and too emotional. So
there was no clapping out for me. My final day ended
with the usual rush of telephone calls, a raft of documents to

be signed and a long walk, alone, down the hall and out the door.

During this walk I considered something that I had not given much thought to in the past. Our aim had been to make South Simcoe a safe haven and a spiritual oasis for the children. We wanted them to know they would be loved, respected and cared for within its shabby old walls. Yet, over my last few years there, I felt that I had been the one who was loved and cared for. If I had become sick, someone would have watched over me; whenever I needed a kind word, someone spoke it for me. I genuinely loved the school, the staff, the students, the community, and all that they represented. I also recognized the changes that had taken place within me. Like the children I, too, had grown. Like them, I had become more resilient. I was both stronger and more centred as a person. The physician, in seeking to heal and care for her patients, found herself also healed and cared for from the same process.

I did not, and still don't, enjoy goodbyes. So that night, filled with a maelstrom of emotions and recalling all that the school had meant to me, I got into my car and drove home.

Times and situations change. Teachers and students alike must understand and accept this fact of life.

When I had been assigned to South Simcoe, it was a place I didn't want to go; now it was a place I didn't want to leave. The children had helped me find a strength I never knew was within me, and I am forever indebted to them for it.

One of the foundations of wisdom, I believe, is the awareness of universal themes, concepts of belief that are equally valid everywhere in the world. Among the most important of these universal themes is the one my father had first taught me when I accompanied him on his visits to distant villages, seeking people who needed assistance. You have to show people where the opportunities in their lives can be found, and explain how to use them. When they grow more confident, they will discover new opportunities for themselves. Then they will assume the role you had undertaken earlier; they too will find opportunities for others—and so the cycle continues.

Respect for self and others is another universal theme. I believe every society must nurture this concept in its children.

Hope may be the most valuable universal theme of all. With hope, children embrace a vision of better things for themselves, and realize that they do not have to settle for the same conditions into which they were born.

We gave the children of South Simcoe a realization of the opportunities available to them; an awareness of the importance of respect for themselves and others; hope that they can continue to grow and seek happiness, success and satisfaction in their lives; and knowledge that these represent the foundation of a strong and safe community.

They gave themselves better grades, a more promising future and a sense of the unlimited potential within them.

The things they gave my staff and me are beyond measure and description.

Acknowledgements

*F*or helping me develop this book, I feel a deep sense of gratitude to my mother, for her love, devotion and continuous demonstrations of love; my children Shiva, Lisa and Rishi, for their support; the loving memory of my father, mother-in-law, sisters-in-law and brother-in-law; my sister Shirley, her husband Winston and my nephew Navin; my brother Naresh, his wife Sue and my rays of sunshine Chantal and Kiran; and to the "Trinidadian Deans" and the "Swiss Deans."

I am also grateful to the following people: the children, staff and community who worked hand-in-hand and heart-to-heart with me to develop the *Together We Light the Way* model; the principals, teachers and support staff who were at South Simcoe long before I was and paved the way for me; the wonderful staff with whom I worked at South Simcoe Public School for their dedication and commitment to the children entrusted to their care (Jane Baier, Doug Beeston, Joanne Blohm, Michael Bowman, Vicky Caruana, Dawn Christiansen, Gisele Cournoyer, Nancy Cregg, Jacki Devolin, Cathie Edwards, Alvena Dunhill, Sarah Dunstall, Debbie Faryna, Tamara Gattie, Jennifer Goodbrand, Joe Hamilton, Anne Hansen, Denise Hoskin, Kim Hutchinson, Janet King,

Sharon McLean, Heather Morrison, Lona O'Reilly, Claudette Oegema, Annette Parker, Andrea Peel, Jane Pelow, Sally Roberts, Dale Shepphard, Heather Stallaert, Joan Strzelczyk, Anne Taylor, Sandy Thomas and Randy Weekes); the many teachers, principals and friends at the Durham District School Board who have given me feedback, encouragement and support; my superintendent Norm Powers and my director Grant Yeo, who gave me the courage to get this book done; Chuck Powers, Don Peel and Dave Snoddon for always being there to guide me; Ken Munroe, Bruce Mather and Pauline Laing, directors of education, who all took time to encourage my work; the supervisory officers (past and present) of the Durham District School Board who helped me in a variety of ways (Dave Brown, Craig Burch, Brian Cain, Casey Daleman, Kaye Egan, Laura Elliott, Bill Fairburn, Bev Freedman, Jack Gardner, Mike Graham, Doug Kettle, George Marlow, Bob Martin, Jack Massie, Don McLean, Trudy Nisbett, Clarence Prins, Ron Trbovich, Barry Vail, Bruce Walker, Doug Wilson and Carol Yeo); the chairpersons and trustees of the Durham District School Board (Ruth Lafarga, Ian Brown, Louise Farr, Patti Bowman, Audrey MacLean, Ruth Ann Schedlich, Doug Ross, Colleen Jordan, Bobbie Drew, Kathleen Hopper, Susan Shetler and Jane Weist); the principals with whom I worked and who encouraged my creativity (Doug Bell, Jack Gardner, Carmen Sarles, Rodger Lappin, Bob Kochan and Bill Kellington); my friends Cathy Barber, Luigia Ayotte, Rita Edwards, Gail Elliot, Pauline Langmaid, Wendy Peyton, Beth Selby, Dianne Serra and Joan Zamora, who helped me through many rough times; Mayor Diamond and her staff; the Durham Regional Police Service; my advisors Eric Newell, Roland Hosein, Rob Pitfield, Bob Ellis, Ken Leithwood, Claude LeGrande, Courtney Garneau,

Barry Kuntz, Tom McNoun and Linda Sinclair; the people who invited me to speak in the Caribbean (Bill Clarke, Bill Robinson, Richard Young, Suruj Rambachand, Michael Viechweg and Helen Drayton); Lynne Schuyler, Daphne Hart, Cynthia Good, Jackie Kaiser and Barbara Berson, for convincing me there was a book; Peter Edwards and John Reynolds, for helping me to put my thoughts together; Carol Slater and Allison Griffith, my two principals at the principals' courses, for giving me the opportunity to be a part of the group; David Onley, Linda Manjuris, Louise Brown, Gail Gallant, Peter Gzowski, Pat Ganase and Joanne Burghardt, who highlighted the development of the *Together We Light the Way* model on TV, radio and in newspaper articles; my friends at the Conference Board of Canada (MaryAnn McLaughlin, Michael Bloom, Linda Scott, Doug Watt and Kurtis Kitagawa); my friends at the Federal Department of Justice (Dana Donovan, Greg McDougall, Michelle Vallee and Patricia Begin); my friends at the International Partnership network for their many invitations to speak and to Betsy Nelson for her kindness; and my *Together We Light the Way* family (Kim Kelly-Whyte, Andrea Peel, Roxann Brown, Marlene Gutsole and Mike Lancaster).